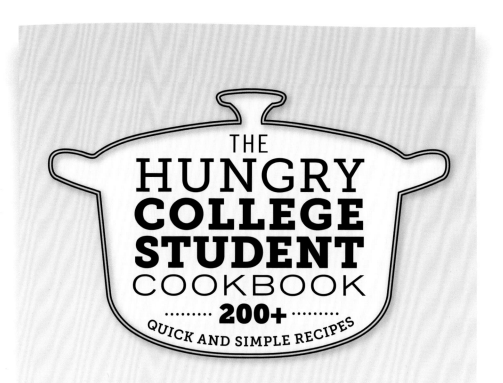

# THE HUNGRY COLLEGE STUDENT COOKBOOK

### 200+
#### QUICK AND SIMPLE RECIPES

spruce

An Hachette UK Company
www.hachette.co.uk

First published in Great Britain in 2019 by Spruce
an imprint of Octopus Publishing Group Ltd
Carmelite House, 50 Victoria Embankment
London EC4Y 0DZ
www.octopusbooks.co.uk
www.octopusbooksusa.com

This material was previously published as *The Hungry Student Cookbook*. Some of the recipes have been previously published by Hamlyn.

Distributed in the US by Hachette Book Group
1290 Avenue of the Americas, 4th and 5th Floors
New York, NY 10104

Distributed in Canada by Canadian Manda Group
664 Annette St., Toronto, Ontario, Canada M6S 2C8

ISBN 978-1-84601-583-0

Printed and bound in China

10 9 8 7 6 5 4 3 2 1

Drinking excessive alcohol can significantly damage your health. The US Department of Health and Human Sciences recommends men do not regularly exceed 1–2 drinks a day and women 1 drink. Never operate a vehicle when you have been drinking alcohol. Octopus Publishing Group accepts no liability or responsibility for any consequences resulting from the use of or reliance upon the information contained herein.

This book includes dishes made with nuts and nut derivatives.

Standard level spoon measurements are used in all recipes.

Ovens should be preheated to the specified temperature — if using a fan-assisted oven, follow the manufacturer's instructions for adjusting the time and the temperature.

# CONTENTS

# INTRODUCTION

You have secured your place on a course, and you have found somewhere to live, and now all that's left to do is pack your bags. Leaving home for the first time is one of the biggest events in anyone's life and, although your folks will probably be on hand to bail you out when you lose your wallet and greet you with open arms when you head home with a sack of dirty washing, you're still taking that first independent leap into the unknown, with all the excitement, uncertainty, and hangovers that it involves.

Whether you're moving into a dormitory or shared housing, you're going to have to start looking after yourself. If you're used to your meals miraculously appearing from the kitchen every night and your clothes being laundered and neatly folded on your bed, this could come as a bit of a shock. It's time to become familiar with household appliances and to learn how to use them without flooding or burning down your building. And there's no excuse: if you can download apps onto a smartphone, you can almost certainly locate and manipulate the controls on a washing machine so that you have some clean undergarments.

## SPACE INVADERS

You may or may not be studying politics, but you're likely to have to use some skills of diplomacy and negotiation when you move in with your housemates. If you're sharing with a bunch of people you don't know – and now have to share a bathroom and kitchen with – then it's going to take a while to set some ground rules so that you can live harmoniously together under one roof.

When it comes to cleaning, one student's den of iniquity is another's homage to cleanliness, and whether you get on with your housemates in the bar is irrelevant when you're faced with a sink full of pasta-encrusted plates and mugs you could donate to medical science. A cleaning rota might sound like a draconian option when you're embarking on a few years of living by your own rules, but it's a good way to name and shame the soap-dodgers and to stop your house from descending into total chaos. When it comes to the point where the only living creatures that want to visit the kitchen are rodents, you will appreciate the benefits of a rota.

## FINDER'S KEEPERS

Different people have different views on food rights. While you might firmly believe that your precious piece of sharp cheddar should be left untouched for when you have a sudden cheese craving, your housemates might have more socialist leanings and believe that all food is up for grabs. Again, you need to decide on an agreed protocol on moving-in day: will all food be fair game, or are you going to allocate refrigerator and cabinet space to each housemate and hold a public enquiry if so much as a square of chocolate is unaccounted for?

If you're living with more than a couple of people, it isn't practicable to traipse off to the supermarket together on a weekly basis. Apart from looking like a bedraggled version of the Von Trapp family huddled around a communal shopping cart, the discussions over ingredients, likes and dislikes, and special offers will eat substantially into your study or social time. It's far better to nominate a "shopper" each week and agree on a basic shopping list for the items that everyone will use (condiments, toilet paper, beans, pasta, bread, milk, and so on). If someone has a penchant for duck liver pâté – or something else that doesn't come under the "essentials" label – they can buy and enjoy it separately.

## DIRTY FILM

We're talking now about the film of scum on your work surfaces, which will soon build up if you don't occasionally run a cloth around your kitchen. It won't take too many late-night food binges or missed ticks on the cleaning rota for your kitchen to degenerate into something squatters would run a mile from. The longer you leave it, the more difficult it will be to clean, and there's a greater likelihood that the area will become a breeding ground for flies, maggots, and curious furry friends.

Here are ten simple tips to help you avoid a trip to hospital.
- Keep food covered so it's protected from pesky flies.
- Keep raw meat covered and on the lowest shelf in the refrigerator, away from other food to prevent contamination.
- Wash your hands before you start preparing food – you might be immune to your own germs, but your housemates won't be.
- Wash fruit and vegetables before you prepare them. Remember that quite a few people will have handled the fruit and veg before they arrive in your kitchen.

- Use scorching hot water for washing dishes and buy yourself a pair of plastic gloves if you can't handle the heat. The hotter the water, the greater likelihood there will be of killing germs.
- Empty garbage cans regularly – they are magnets for bugs, especially in the summer.
- Try not to leave food out (and yes, that even includes dirty plates, even when you're really tired) because the smell can attract mice and flies.
- Defrost meat in the refrigerator, rather than leaving it out on work surfaces.
- Put dish towels and cloths in the laundry regularly – they are another breeding ground for germs.
- If something looks or smells bad, don't eat it (unless, of course, like Camembert, the bad smell is part of its culinary charm).

## HONE YOUR TECHNIQUE

If you have spent much of your life avoiding the kitchen, except to eat, then it's time to roll up your sleeves and get to grips with a few basic cooking techniques. Nothing wows a potential mate like the sight of someone expertly chopping garlic and juggling pans without breaking into a sweat. Even if you learn how to prepare only a couple of key recipes, you know you've always got something up your sleeve for a romantic night in or for a rowdy, food-based gathering with your mates. If you are a complete novice when it comes to the kitchen, here are a few terms and techniques to give your culinary confidence a boost.

### Pare

This isn't to be confused with the fruit! It's the

way you peel the skin from a piece of fruit or a vegetable, using a paring knife.

## Beat
If you want fluffy eggs you're going to have to beat the hell out of them. You need a firm arm, a good wrist movement, and a lot of patience for this. You can use a fork for scrambling or a food whisk if you're trying to create magic by transforming sloppy egg whites into fluffy clouds.

## Marinate
If you leave your fish fillets or chicken portions to soak in a sauce for a while before cooking them, congratulations – you've just marinated. It's a way of getting extra flavor into your food, and can be anything from olive oil and lemon juice to jerk seasoning or barbecue sauce.

## Baste
Here you marinate the meat first then brush it with the marinade while it's cooking. It helps to add flavor and keep the meat moist.

## Season
Seasoning is mainly about adding salt and pepper to a recipe for maximum flavor. The key is to add a little at a time and taste as you go along. You can also season with spices and other condiments – the recipes will let you know what you need.

## Puree
This is mash with muscles and the only way to guarantee you don't end up with lumps in your spuds. You can push the cooked potatoes through a sieve or use a food processor. You can also puree other vegetables, such as carrots or peas, for classy side dishes that are easy to whip up.

## Chop
This is just another word for "cut," but some things need to be chopped into big chunks, while other ingredients require a more delicate and precise hand. If real precision is called for, chop becomes "dice."

## Poach
You've probably come across a poached egg before (if not, you really shouldn't be left unsupervised with raw ingredients and sharp knives), but you can also poach fish and chicken. It's a gentle way of cooking food in water, milk, or other liquid so that it stays moist and tender.

## Simmer
Liquid that's bubbling over the side of the pan can be quite aggressive toward delicate food, but simmering treats food with a little more respect. Simmering should stop your boiled eggs from cracking and your sauces from burning on the bottom of the pan.

## Fillet
The butcher, fish merchants or supermarket will have generally done this way before you get to the stage of handling your ingredients, but if you really want a second date make sure your prospective partner is idling in the kitchen while you skilfully remove the fillets from a mackerel.

## Blanch
Involves giving your vegetables the merest hint of contact with a pan of boiling water. Cook vegetables like broccoli and carrots for just a few minutes to retain more of their nutrients and taste better too. (Let's leave the over-boiled, gray vegetable medley to nursing homes, shall we?)

## SITTING ON THE SHELF
There are some basic ingredients that crop up time and again in recipes so it makes sense to have a stockpile of these in your cupboard. That way, you will always have the makings of something nutritious. Condiments, sauces, dried herbs, and spices last a long time so it's worth making a list before you move in and getting everyone to buy a few things to give your pantry a boost. Here's what every self-respecting kitchen should contain:

### Salt and pepper
Fine and ground respectively for everyday, or sea salt and peppercorns to impress.

### Diced tomatoes

These are essential for sauces, soups, and stews. They are cheap, nutritious, and versatile.

### Oil

Vegetable oil is the budget go-to oil of choice, but olive oil doesn't cost much more and it's great for dressings, marinades, and sauces as well as for cooking.

### Butter (or spread)

Because toast provides a disproportionate number of the average student's daily calories, you must always have a supply of spread ... and whatever else you like to slather on your bread.

### Onions and garlic

These vegetables are the basics of pretty much every Indian and Italian soup, curry, and sauce. They add heaps of flavor and are also good for battling colds and bugs.

### Rice

When there's nothing fresh in the refrigerator you can always rustle up a plate of spicy rice. Choose brown for health, arborio for risottos, and jasmine for Thai food.

### Pasta

It's a cliché, but many a student has avoided malnutrition thanks to a sturdy pasta jar. Pick one or two types – spaghetti and penne, for instance – so that you don't end up with loads of almost empty bags of random shapes.

### Cans of beans

You don't need to stick to baked beans. Broaden your culinary horizons by stocking up on other cheap, protein-rich varieties like kidney beans (great for chili), cranberry and lima beans (for adding bulk to soups), and chickpeas (perfect for stews, curries, and salads).

### Canned fish

Another must-have staple. You can live through nuclear fallout if you've got enough cans of tuna and salmon in your pantry. Think baked potatoes, pasta, salads, and sandwiches.

### Sugar

No need to waste precious cash on superfine sugar; make your own by blending granulated sugar for a second or two in a food processor.

## GOING GOURMET

As you pick your way through this book, you will first be mystified, then intrigued and eventually (we hope) fluent in cookery speak. The recipes have been designed to treat you with the brains you were born with. They assume that the fact you've arrived at college means you have some previous knowledge of books and the modicum of intelligence required to follow a set of simple instructions through to their delicious conclusion.

It's time to buck the trend of generations of kitchen-shy students who survived on cold beans and treat yourself and your housemates to decent dinners. Good luck and enjoy.

### BUDGETING

Boring as it may be, unless you want to spend the last month of each semester hiding in your hovel and eating plain rice, budgeting is a necessary part of student life. Each recipe in this book is rated from 1 to 3, with 1s providing end-of-semester saviors that can be scraped together for a pittance, and 3s to splash out and impress all your friends.

YELLOW CURRY CHICKEN
WITH PINEAPPLE

TUNA ARRABIATA

MAPLE-GLAZED CHICKEN

# PhD
## IN ONE POT

CHICKEN & SPINACH MASALA

# CHUNKY CHORIZO, PASTA & BEAN SOUP

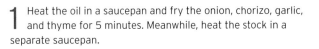

¼ cup extra virgin olive oil
1 large onion, chopped
2 oz chorizo sausage, chopped
4 garlic cloves, crushed
2 tablespoons chopped thyme
3 cups Chicken Stock (see page 234)
5 cups canned tomatoes, sieved
2 13-oz each cans cranberry beans, rinsed and drained
7 oz small pasta shapes, such as conchigliette
3 tablespoons chopped basil
salt and pepper
grated Parmesan cheese, to serve

Serves **4**
Prep time **10 minutes**
Cooking time **30 minutes**

**1** Heat the oil in a saucepan and fry the onion, chorizo, garlic, and thyme for 5 minutes. Meanwhile, heat the stock in a separate saucepan.

**2** Add the hot stock, tomatoes, beans, and salt and pepper to the onion mixture and bring to a boil. Reduce the heat, cover, and simmer for 15 minutes.

**3** Stir in the pasta and basil and cook for an additional 8–10 minutes until the pasta is tender. Adjust the seasoning if necessary, then spoon into warmed bowls and serve topped with grated Parmesan.

AFFORDABILITY 2

# SMOKED **HADDOCK** CHOWDER

AFFORDABILITY
2

1 Cut the tops off the bread rolls and pull out the soft centers, leaving a bowl shape and a lid. Place on a baking sheet in a preheated oven, 325°F, and bake for 25 minutes until they have dried out and become crispy. Brush the inside of the bread rolls with the egg. Put the rolls back in the oven for 5 more minutes to dry out once again. Remove from the oven and set aside.

2 Heat the butter in a large saucepan, add the green onions and fry until soft. Add the garlic and potatoes and fry for a minute more. Pour in the milk, cream, and stock and bring the soup to a boil, then reduce the heat and simmer for 10 minutes or until the potatoes are almost cooked.

3 Add the corn and smoked haddock to the pan and simmer for an additional 5 minutes until the fish has cooked. Season with salt and pepper.

4 Heat the oil in a skillet and fry the bacon until crispy. When ready to serve, place the bread bowls in shallow bowls. Pour the soup into the bread bowls, then top with the bacon and a sprinkling of parsley.

4 large round white bread rolls
1 egg, lightly beaten
4 tablespoons butter
8 green onions, chopped
1 garlic clove, crushed
2 large, waxy potatoes, peeled and cubed
1½ cups milk
scant 1 cup whipping cream
scant 1 cup Fish Stock (see page 235)
1 8-oz can corn kernels, drained
1 lb smoked haddock, skinned and cut into large chunks
1 tablespoon olive oil
8 slices bacon, chopped
salt and pepper
2 tablespoons chopped parsley, to garnish

Serves **4**
Prep time **15 minutes**
Cooking time **30 minutes**

3 tablespoons olive oil
1 onion, finely chopped
2 celery sticks, thinly sliced
2 garlic cloves, thinly sliced
2 14-oz each cans lima beans,
  rinsed and drained
¼ cup sundried tomato paste
3¾ cups Vegetable Stock (see
  page 235)
1 tablespoon chopped rosemary or
  thyme, plus extra to serve
salt and pepper
Parmesan cheese shavings,
  to serve

Serves **4**
Prep time **5 minutes**
Cooking time **20 minutes**

# LIMA BEAN
# *&* SUNDRIED
# TOMATO SOUP

1 Heat the oil in a saucepan, add the onion and fry for
  3 minutes until softened. Add the celery and garlic and fry
for 2 minutes.

2 Add the lima beans, tomato paste, stock, rosemary or
  thyme, and a little salt and pepper. Bring to a boil, then
reduce the heat, cover, and simmer gently for 15 minutes. Serve
sprinkled with the Parmesan shavings.

# ROAST ROOT VEGETABLE SOUP

**1** Put the carrots and parsnips in a roasting pan, spray lightly with olive oil, and season with salt and pepper. Roast in a preheated oven, 400°F, for 1 hour or until the vegetables are very soft.

**2** Meanwhile, 20 minutes before the vegetables have finished roasting, put the leeks in a large saucepan with the stock and 1 teaspoon of the thyme. Cover the pan and simmer for 20 minutes.

**3** Transfer the roasted root vegetables to a blender or food processor and blend, adding a little of the stock if necessary. Transfer to the stock saucepan and season to taste. Add the remaining thyme, stir, and simmer for 5 minutes to reheat.

**4** Ladle into individual bowls and serve garnished with the thyme sprigs.

4 carrots, chopped
2 parsnips, chopped
olive oil, for spraying
1 leek, finely chopped
5 cups Vegetable Stock (see page 235)
2 teaspoons thyme leaves
salt and pepper
thyme sprigs, to garnish

Serves **6**
Prep time **10 minutes**
Cooking time **1 hour 5 minutes**

AFFORDABILITY
**1**

# CHEAT'S CURRIED VEGETABLE SOUP

2 tablespoons sunflower oil
1 onion, finely chopped
2 garlic cloves, finely chopped
4 teaspoons mild curry paste
1-inch piece of fresh ginger root, peeled and grated
2 small baking potatoes, diced
2 carrots, diced
1 small cauliflower, core discarded, florets cut into small pieces
1/3 cup red lentils
6 1/4 cups Vegetable or Chicken Stock (see pages 234 and 235)
1 14 1/2-oz can diced tomatoes
4 cups spinach leaves, rinsed, and any large leaves torn into pieces
naan bread, to serve (optional)

**Raita**
2/3 cup low-fat plain yogurt
4 tablespoons chopped cilantro leaves
4 teaspoons mango chutney

Serves **6**
Prep time **25 minutes**
Cooking time **40 minutes**

AFFORDABILITY 1

1 Heat the oil in a large saucepan, add the onion, and fry for 5 minutes, stirring until softened. Stir in the garlic, curry paste, and ginger and cook for 1 minute.

2 Mix in the potatoes, carrots, cauliflower, and lentils. Pour in the stock and tomatoes, season with salt and pepper, and bring to a boil. Cover and simmer for 30 minutes or until the lentils are tender.

3 Meanwhile, make the raita. Mix together the yogurt, cilantro, and mango chutney and spoon into a small bowl.

4 Add the spinach to the soup and cook for 2 minutes until just wilted. Taste and adjust the seasoning if needed. Ladle the soup into shallow bowls and top with spoonfuls of raita. Serve with warmed naan bread, if desired.

# MAPLE-GLAZED
## *Chicken*

4 chicken thigh and drumstick joints
2 dessert apples, cored, quartered
8 oz shallots, peeled, halved if large
1¼ lb parsnips, quartered
6 bay leaves
2 tablespoons olive oil
2 tablespoons maple syrup
2 tablespoons cider vinegar
salt and pepper
arugula salad, to serve (optional)

Serves **4**
Prep time **15 minutes**
Cooking time **40-45 minutes**

**1** Slash the chicken joints 3-4 times and put them into a large roasting pan with the apples, shallots, parsnips, and bay leaves.

**2** Mix the remaining ingredients together and spoon over the chicken and vegetables. Add ¼ cup water to the base of the pan. Cook in a preheated oven, 375°F, for 40-45 minutes, spooning the glaze over the chicken once or twice until deep brown and cooked through.

**3** Spoon onto plates and serve with an arugula salad, if desired.

AFFORDABILITY 2

# CHICKEN WITH CORNMEAL DUMPLINGS

1 Heat the oil in a large, shallow flameproof casserole and fry the chicken pieces for about 5 minutes until lightly browned. Stir in the spice blend and cook for another minute. Drain to a plate.

2 Add the onion, bacon, and peppers and fry, stirring frequently, for 10 minutes or until beginning to color.

3 Return the chicken to the casserole and stir in the stock and a little seasoning. Bring to a boil, cover with a lid, and bake in a preheated oven, 350°F, for 45 minutes until the chicken is tender.

4 To prepare the dumplings, mix together the flour, cornmeal, red pepper flakes, cilantro, and cheese in a bowl. Beat the butter with the egg and milk and add to the bowl. Mix together to make a thick paste that is fairly sticky but holds its shape.

5 Stir the tomatoes and cream into the chicken mixture and season to taste. Put spoonfuls of the dumpling mixture over the top. Return to the oven, uncovered, for an additional 30 minutes or until the dumplings have slightly risen and formed a firm crust.

3 tablespoons olive oil
8 boneless, skinless chicken thighs, cut into small pieces
4 teaspoons Cajun spice blend
1 large onion, sliced
3½ oz smoked bacon, chopped
2 red bell peppers, seeded and roughly chopped
2 yellow bell peppers, seeded and roughly chopped
scant 1 cup Chicken Stock (see page 234)
4 small tomatoes, skinned and quartered
scant ½ cup whipping cream
salt and pepper

**Dumplings**
1 cup self-rising flour
²/₃ cup cornmeal
½ teaspoon dried red pepper flakes
3 tablespoons chopped cilantro
²/₃ cup grated cheddar cheese
4 tablespoons butter, melted
1 egg
scant ½ cup milk

Serves **4**
Prep time **25 minutes**
Cooking time **1½ hours**

# CHICKEN KORMA

2 tablespoons sunflower oil
8 boneless, skinless chicken
  thighs, about 2 lb in total, cubed
2 onions, finely chopped, plus
  extra to garnish
1-2 green chiles (to taste), seeded
  and finely chopped
1-inch piece of fresh ginger root,
  peeled and finely chopped
¼ cup plus 1 tablespoon korma
  curry paste
1 cup coconut cream or milk
1¼ cups Chicken Stock (see page
  234)
2 tablespoons ground almonds
small bunch of cilantro
scant 1 cup plain yogurt
2 tomatoes, diced
salt and pepper
chapattis, to serve

**1** Heat the oil in a large skillet, add the chicken a few pieces at time until it is all in the pan and fry, stirring, until golden. Remove from the pan with a slotted spoon and transfer to a flameproof casserole.

**2** Add the onions, green chiles, ginger, and curry paste to the pan and fry, stirring, for 2-3 minutes. Pour in the coconut cream or milk, stock, and ground almonds. Tear half the cilantro into pieces and add to the sauce with a little salt and pepper. Bring to a boil, stirring, then spoon over the chicken. Cover with the lid and cook over a low heat for 30-40 minutes or until the chicken is cooked through.

**3** Stir the korma then ladle into bowls, top with spoonfuls of yogurt, tomatoes, and extra raw onion and the remaining cilantro torn into small pieces. Serve with warm chapattis.

Serves **4**
Prep time **20 minutes**
Cooking time **45-55 minutes**

## Cool down your curry

If you get a bit carried away with your chiles, and you've made a curry that will blow your mates' heads off, don't despair. Remove some of the sauce (you can freeze this for next time) and add a can of diced tomatoes, some coconut milk, or plain yogurt to the remaining sauce.

AFFORDABILITY
2

# YELLOW CURRY **CHICKEN** WITH PINEAPPLE

CHICKEN AND PINEAPPLE IS A TYPICALLY THAI COMBINATION, WHICH GOES WELL WITH YELLOW CURRY IN BOTH COLOR AND FLAVOR.

**1** To make the curry paste, soak the chopped chiles in hot water for 2 minutes and drain. Use a mortar and pestle to grind the chiles and lemon grass together, then add the remaining ingredients and blend to make a smooth paste.

**2** Heat the oil in a nonstick wok or large skillet and stir-fry the curry paste for 2 minutes or until it is fragrant.

**3** Add the chicken and stir-fry for 4-5 minutes. Add the coconut milk, stock, pineapple, and fish sauce and heat through. Spoon into a serving bowl, garnish with the sliced chiles, and serve immediately with rice, if desired.

1½ tablespoons sunflower oil
10 oz skinless chicken breast fillet, thinly sliced
scant 1 cup coconut milk, shaken well
scant 1 cup Chicken Stock (see page 234)
10 oz pineapple, cut into 1-inch cubes (about 1½ cups)
1½ tablespoons fish sauce (nam pla)
1 long red chile, stemmed, seeded, and finely sliced, to garnish

**Yellow curry paste**
2-3 dried, long red chiles or 5 dried small red chiles, seeded and chopped
2 lemon grass stalks, finely sliced
2 garlic cloves, chopped
3 shallots, chopped
1 tablespoon yellow curry powder
1 teaspoon ground coriander
1 teaspoon ground cumin

Serves **2**
Prep time **30 minutes**
Cooking time **10-15 minutes**

AFFORDABILITY **2**

2 tablespoons oil
1 onion, thinly sliced
2 garlic cloves, crushed
1 green chile, seeded and thinly
  sliced
1 teaspoon finely grated fresh
  ginger root
1 teaspoon ground coriander
1 teaspoon ground cumin
1 7-oz can tomatoes
1½ lb boneless, skinless chicken
  thighs, cut into bite-size
  chunks
scant 1 cup sour cream
6 cups spinach, roughly
  chopped
2 tablespoons chopped cilantro
salt and pepper

Serves **4**
Prep time **15 minutes**
Cooking time **13-16 minutes**

# CHICKEN & SPINACH MASALA

**1** Heat the oil in a large, heavy saucepan, add the onion, garlic, chile, and ginger and stir-fry for 2-3 minutes. Add the ground coriander and cumin, stir, and cook for another minute.

**2** Pour in the tomatoes and cook gently for 3 minutes. Increase the heat, add the chicken and cook, stirring, until the outside of the chicken is sealed. Stir in the sour cream and spinach.

**3** Cover the pan and cook the chicken mixture gently for 6-8 minutes, stirring occasionally. Stir in the chopped cilantro, season to taste, and serve.

# CARIBBEAN CHICKEN
# WITH RICE & PEAS

**1** Remove the skin from the chicken thighs, slash each thigh two or three times and rub with the jerk marinade.

**2** Heat 1 tablespoon oil in a large skillet, add the chicken, and fry over a high heat until browned on both sides. Lift out with a slotted spoon and transfer to a plate. Add the remaining oil, the onions, and garlic, reduce the heat and fry for 5 minutes or until softened and lightly browned. Pour in the coconut milk and stock, season with salt and pepper, and bring to a boil.

**3** Transfer the mixture to a flameproof casserole and add the chicken and beans. Stir to mix, cover, cook over a low heat for 20 minutes until the chicken is cooked through and tender.

**4** Stir in the rice, replace the lid, and cook over a high heat for 15 minutes. Add the frozen peas (no need to thaw) and cook for an additional 5 minutes. Spoon onto plates and serve garnished with lime wedges and cilantro sprigs.

8 chicken thighs, about 2 lb in total
3 tablespoons jerk marinade
2 tablespoons sunflower oil
2 large onions, chopped
2 garlic cloves, finely chopped
1 2/3 cups full-fat coconut milk
1 1/4 cups Chicken Stock (see page 234)
1 15-oz can red kidney beans, drained
1 cup easy-cook long grain rice
2/3 cup frozen peas
salt and pepper

**To garnish**
lime wedges
cilantro sprigs

Serves **4**
Prep time **20 minutes**
Cooking time **55-60 minutes**

# SAUSAGE & SWEET POTATO HASH

3 tablespoons olive oil
8 pork sausages
3 large red onions, thinly sliced
1 teaspoon sugar
1 lb sweet potatoes, scrubbed and
   cut into small chunks
8 sage leaves
2 tablespoons balsamic vinegar
salt and pepper

Serves **4**
Prep time **15 minutes**
Cooking time **45 minutes**

**1** Heat the oil in a large skillet or flameproof casserole and fry the sausages, turning frequently, for about 10 minutes or until browned. Drain to a plate.

**2** Add the onions and sugar to the pan and cook gently, stirring frequently, until lightly browned. Return the sausages to the pan and add the sweet potatoes, sage leaves, and a little seasoning.

**3** Cover the pan with a lid or kitchen foil and cook over a very gentle heat for about 25 minutes until the potatoes are tender.

**4** Drizzle with the vinegar, check the seasoning, and serve.

# BEST
## BRAIN FOOD

You got a place at a university so you must have some gray matter floating around between your ears and, whether you're studying medicine or the benefits of floatation techniques, at least you've made it. However, with thousands of brain cells irreversibly zapped every time you have a big night at the student union, it makes sense to try to preserve those that remain with a few food wins. Here are some of the ingredients that will give you the edge in the lecture theater.

### OILY FISH

Unfortunately, fish sticks won't cut the mustard: we're talking about salmon, mackerel, and tuna if you really want to give your brain a boost. It's the omega 3 acids that you're after, but don't worry if you've got a fish phobia—it's the easiest food in the world to cook. Try Tuna & Pasta Bake (see page 134) for a tasty meal to get you hooked or add some salmon flakes or tuna to sandwiches, pasta sauces, or baked potatoes.

### NUTS & SEEDS

This is where you can get a quick, tasty burst of vitamin E, which helps to protect your cells. Buy a big mixed bag and transfer a handful at a time to a freezer bag or small plastic tub for a daily snack when you're out and about.

## WHOLEGRAINS

Unfortunately, you really should try to avoid cheap white bread and shuffle up next to the healthy shoppers in the whole-wheat section instead. When it comes to bread, the more grains the better, and switching to brown rice and whole-wheat pasta, or to porridge for breakfast, will make sure you get plenty of fiber, vitamins, and slow-burning carbs into your diet.

## EGGS

As they are a student staple, you probably have a fair number of eggs in your diet already, but isn't it nice to know that they're good for your brain too? For extra points, try getting your eggs by poaching, boiling, or scrambling them rather than in a fry-up at your local greasy spoon.

## CHOCOLATE

This isn't an excuse to swap meals for candy, but when it comes to chocolate a little of what you fancy really does do you good. You need to be a bit discerning in your buying habits though, because it's bittersweet chocolate that has the most antioxidants and flavonoids (technical terms for healthy things). But don't forget that all chocolate contains heaps of sugar so you need to rein in your sweet tooth and treat it, well, like a treat.

# EASY
## SAUSAGE
*&* BEANS

1 tablespoon sunflower oil
1 onion, chopped
½ teaspoon smoked paprika
2 13½-oz each cans baked beans
2 teaspoons whole-grain mustard
2 tablespoons Worcestershire
  sauce
¼ cup plus 2 tablespoons
  Vegetable Stock (see page 235)
2 tomatoes, roughly chopped
½ red bell pepper, cored, seeded
  and diced
11½ oz chilled frankfurters, thickly
  sliced
salt and pepper
buttered toast, to serve

**1** Heat the oil in a skillet, add the onion and fry, stirring, for 5 minutes or until softened and just beginning to turn golden.

**2** Stir in the paprika and cook for 1 minute, then mix in the beans, mustard, Worcestershire sauce, and stock. Bring to a boil, then stir in the tomatoes, bell pepper, and a little salt and pepper.

**3** Put the frankfurters in a flameproof casserole and tip the baked bean mixture over the top. Cover with the lid and cook over a low heat for 40-45 minutes, stirring occasionally.

**4** Stir well, spoon into shallow bowls, and serve with buttered toast fingers.

Serves **4**
Prep time **15 minutes**
Cooking time **50-55 minutes**

# Creamy Pork & CIDER HOTPOT

**1** Cut the pork into small pieces, discarding any excess fat. Season the flour with a little salt and use to coat the meat.

**2** Melt the butter with the oil in a shallow, flameproof casserole and gently fry the pork, in batches, until lightly browned, draining each batch to a plate.

**3** Add the onion and leek to the casserole and fry gently for 5 minutes. Return the meat to the pan, along with the cider, sage, and mustard. Bring just to a boil, cover with a lid, reduce the heat, and cook on the lowest setting for 30 minutes.

**4** Stir the sour cream into the sauce and put the pear slices on top. Arrange the sweet potato slices in overlapping layers on top, putting the end pieces underneath and keeping the best slices for the top layer. Brush with the chili oil and sprinkle with salt.

**5** Cook in a preheated oven, 325ºF, for 45 minutes or until the potatoes are tender and lightly browned. Sprinkle with the chopped parsley before serving.

1¼ lb lean, boneless pork leg
2 teaspoons all-purpose flour
2 tablespoons butter
1 tablespoon oil
1 small onion, chopped
1 large leek, chopped
scant 2 cups hard cider
1 tablespoon chopped sage
2 tablespoons grainy mustard
scant ½ cup sour cream
2 pears, peeled, cored and thickly
  sliced
14½ oz sweet potatoes, scrubbed
  and thinly sliced
2 tablespoons chili-infused oil
salt
chopped parsley, to garnish

Serves **4**
Prep time **25 minutes**
Cooking time **1½ hours**

AFFORDABILITY
**2**

# Cassoulet

AFFORDABILITY 3

IN A GOOD CASSOULET THE BEANS TURN SOFT AND CREAMY AND THICKEN THE MEATY JUICES.

3 cups dried navy beans, soaked overnight in water
¼ cup olive oil or goose fat
1½ lb piece of bacon, cut into chunks
4 duck legs, halved
8 garlicky sausages
2 onions, chopped
2 bay leaves
5 cups Chicken Stock (see page 234)
4 garlic cloves, crushed
good pinch of ground cloves
3 tablespoons tomato paste
1½ cups fresh bread crumbs
salt and pepper

Serves **6**
Prep time **30 minutes, plus soaking**
Cooking time **about 3½ hours**

**1** Drain the beans and put them in a large saucepan. Cover them with cold water, bring to a boil, and cook rapidly for 10 minutes. Reduce the heat and simmer gently for 30 minutes until slightly softened. Drain.

**2** Heat the oil or fat in a large, heavy skillet, add the pork pieces and fry, in batches, until lightly browned. Drain and fry the duck pieces and sausages until browned.

**3** Tip half the beans into a large earthenware pot or casserole dish and sprinkle with half the meat, half the chopped onions, and the bay leaves. Add the remaining beans, meat, and onions.

**4** Blend the stock with the garlic, cloves, and tomato paste and pour the mixture over the beans. Season to taste. Top up with a little water so that the beans are nearly submerged, cover, and cook in a preheated oven, 325°F, for 2 hours until the beans are completely tender.

**5** Sprinkle the bread crumbs over the surface and return to the oven, uncovered, for an additional 30-40 minutes until golden.

# *Spaghetti* CARBONARA

1 Heat the oil in a saucepan, add the bacon, and cook gently for 3 minutes. Add the garlic and cook for another minute.

2 Bring a large saucepan of salted water to a boil and cook the spaghetti for 3-4 minutes if fresh or 8 minutes if dried or according to the package directions. Drain and return the pasta to the pan.

3 Beat the cream and egg yolks together in a bowl, add to the bacon, and mix well over a low heat.

4 Add the sauce and Parmesan to the pasta, season with salt and pepper, and toss well. Serve immediately.

1 tablespoon olive oil
6 oz smoked bacon, rinded and cut into strips
1 garlic clove, crushed
10 oz spaghetti
¼ cup whipping cream
3 egg yolks
¾ cup grated Parmesan cheese
salt and pepper

Serves **4**
Prep time **10 minutes**
Cooking time **15 minutes**

AFFORDABILITY
**2**

### Bin the brands

You might be used to your mom spoiling you with expensive beans and cereal but you've got to fend for yourself now — beans or beer? If you switch to supermarket own-brand ingredients you could save a fortune on your shopping bills. Often, own-brand ingredients taste just as good as branded ones, but it will take some trial and error to find out which brands you're happy to bin and which you simply can't live without.

AFFORDABILITY
2

# Chili
# CON CARNE

2 tablespoons olive oil
1 red onion, finely chopped
3 garlic cloves, finely chopped
8 oz lean gound beef
½ teaspoon ground cumin
1 small red bell pepper, seeded and
   diced
1 14½-oz can diced tomatoes
1 tablespoon tomato paste
2 teaspoons mild chili powder
scant 1 cup Beef Stock (see page
   234)
1 15-oz can red kidney beans,
   rinsed and drained
salt and pepper
brown rice, to serve

Serves **2**
Prep time **15 minutes**
Cooking time **45 minutes**

**1** Heat the oil in a saucepan, add the onion and garlic, and cook for 5 minutes or until beginning to soften. Add the beef and cumin and cook for an additional 5-6 minutes or until browned all over.

**2** Stir in the bell pepper, tomatoes, tomato paste, chili powder, and stock and bring to a boil. Reduce the heat and simmer gently for 30 minutes.

**3** Add the beans and cook for 5 minutes more. Season to taste and serve with brown rice, cooked according to the package directions.

# BOLOGNESE SAUCE

COMBINING ITALIAN-STYLE SPICY SAUSAGES WITH THE MORE FAMILIAR GROUND BEEF GIVES THIS SAUCE A RICH MEATY FLAVOR REMINISCENT OF THE TRADITIONAL SAUCE SERVED IN BOLOGNA.

1 Melt the butter with the oil in a large, heavy saucepan and gently fry the onion and celery for 5 minutes. Add the garlic, beef, and sausages and cook until they are lightly colored, breaking up the beef and the sausages with a wooden spoon.

2 Add the wine and let it bubble for 1–2 minutes until slightly evaporated. Add the tomatoes, sugar, bay leaves, oregano, tomato paste, and a little salt and pepper and bring just to a boil. Reduce the heat to its lowest setting, cover the pan with a lid, and cook for about 1 hour, stirring occasionally, until thick and pulpy.

2 tablespoons butter
2 tablespoons olive oil
1 onion, finely chopped
2 celery sticks, finely chopped
2 garlic cloves, crushed
1 lb lean ground beef
7 oz spicy Italian sausages, skinned
1¼ cups red or white wine
1 14½-oz can diced tomatoes
1 teaspoon sugar
2 bay leaves
1 teaspoon dried oregano
2 tablespoons sun-dried tomato paste
salt and pepper

Serves **4-5**
Prep time **15 minutes**
Cooking time **1¼ hours**

AFFORDABILITY

# STEAK & ALE
## CASEROLE

2 tablespoons all-purpose flour
2 lb braising steak, cut into chunks
2 tablespoons butter
1 tablespoon oil
2 onions, chopped
2 celery sticks, sliced
several thyme sprigs
2 bay leaves
1⅔ cups strong ale
1¼ cups Beef Stock (see page 234)
2 tablespoons molasses
1 lb parsnips, peeled and cut into
    wedges
salt and pepper

Serves **5-6**
Prep time **20 minutes**
Cooking time **1¾ hours**

**1** Season the flour with salt and pepper and coat the beef in the flour. Melt the butter with the oil in a large, flameproof casserole and fry the beef, in batches, until deep brown. Drain with a slotted spoon while you cook the remainder.

**2** Add the onions and celery and fry gently for 5 minutes. Return the beef to the pan and add the herbs, ale, stock, and molasses. Bring just to a boil, reduce the heat, and cover with a lid. Bake in a preheated oven, 325°F, for 1 hour.

**3** Add the parsnips to the dish and return to the oven for 30 minutes more or until the beef and parsnips are tender. Check the seasoning and serve.

# STIFADO

**1** Mix together the pepper, allspice, and rosemary and rub the mixture over the rabbit.

**2** Heat the oil in a large, flameproof casserole and fry the meat, in batches, on all sides until thoroughly browned. Drain the meat to a plate.

**3** Add the onions to the pan with the sugar and fry, stirring frequently, for about 15 minutes until caramelized. Stir in the garlic and cook for a minute more.

**4** Add the vinegar and wine to the pan. Bring to a boil and continue to boil until the mixture has reduced by about one-third. Stir in the tomato paste and a little salt and return the meat to the pan.

**5** Cover with a lid and place in a preheated oven, 300°F, for about 2 hours until the meat is very tender and the juices thick and glossy. Check the seasoning and sprinkle with the parsley before serving.

½ teaspoon ground black pepper
½ teaspoon ground allspice
2 teaspoons finely chopped
  rosemary
1 rabbit, about 1½–1¾ lb, jointed
3 tablespoons olive oil
3 large onions, sliced
2 teaspoons sugar
3 garlic cloves, crushed
⅓ cup red wine vinegar
1¼ cups red wine
3 tablespoons tomato paste
salt
flat leaf parsley, to garnish

Serves **3-4**
Prep time **20 minutes**
Cooking time **2½ hours**

AFFORDABILITY
3

# TUNA
# ARRABIATA

1 tablespoon olive oil
1 onion, chopped
2 garlic cloves, finely chopped
1 red bell pepper, cored, seeded
   and diced
1 teaspoon smoked paprika
¼–½ teaspoon dried red pepper
   flakes
1 s tomatoes
⅔ cup Vegetable or Fish Stock
   (see page 235)
1 7-oz can tuna in water, drained
12 oz spaghetti
salt and pepper

**To serve**
grated Parmesan cheese
basil leaves

Serves **4**
Prep time **20 minutes**
Cooking time **20-25 minutes**

**1** Heat the oil in a skillet, add the onion and fry, stirring, for 5 minutes or until just beginning to turn golden around the edges.

**2** Stir in the garlic, bell pepper, paprika, and dried pepper flakes and cook for 2 minutes. Add the tomatoes, stock, and a little salt and pepper. Bring to a boil, then transfer to a flameproof casserole. Break the tuna into large pieces and stir into the tomato mixture. Cover with the lid and cook over a low heat for 10-15 minutes.

**3** When you are almost ready to serve, bring a large saucepan of salted water to a boil, add the spaghetti, and cook for about 8 minutes until tender or according to the package directions. Drain and stir into the tomato sauce to coat the pasta. Spoon into shallow bowls and sprinkle with grated Parmesan and basil leaves to taste.

# SPINACH & MUSHROOM
## *Lasagna*

1 Make the sauce. Put the milk and bay leaves in a saucepan and heat to boiling point. Remove from the heat and allow to infuse for 20 minutes. Discard the bay leaves.

2 Melt the butter in a separate saucepan, add the flour, and cook over a medium heat, stirring constantly, for 1 minute. Gradually stir in the milk and continue to cook, stirring, until the mixture boils. Reduce the heat and simmer for 2 minutes. Remove from the heat, add most of the cheddar, and stir until melted.

3 Meanwhile, heat the oil in a skillet, add the garlic, thyme, mushrooms, and salt and pepper and cook over a medium heat, stirring frequently, for 5 minutes until tender. Squeeze out the excess water from the spinach and roughly chop. Stir into the mushroom mixture, then remove from the heat.

4 Lightly oil a 2½-quart lasagna dish with spray oil. Spread a quarter of the cheese sauce over the base and add one-third of the mushroom and spinach mixture and one-third of the lasagna sheets. Repeat these layers twice more. Add a final layer of sauce to cover the lasagna and sprinkle with the remaining cheese. Bake in a preheated oven, 375ºF, for 35-40 minutes until browned.

¼ cup olive oil
2 garlic cloves, crushed
2 teaspoons chopped thyme
6 cups trimmed and sliced white
   mushrooms
1 lb frozen leaf spinach (thawed)
spray oil, for oiling
7 oz fresh lasagna sheets
salt and black pepper

**Cheese sauce**
5 cups milk
2 fresh bay leaves
4 tablespoons unsalted butter,
   plus extra for greasing
scant ½ cup all-purpose flour
2¼ cups grated cheddar cheese

Serves **6-8**
Prep time **35 minutes, plus infusing**
Cooking time **45-50 minutes**

# SPINACH & GREEN BEAN
# RISOTTO

4 cups vegetable stock
¼ lb (1 stick) butter
1 tablespoon olive oil
1 garlic clove, crushed and
  chopped
1 onion, finely diced
1½ cups arborio or carnaroli rice
1 cup trimmed green beans, cut
  into short lengths
⅔ cup shelled peas
¾ cup shelled fava beans
1 cup trimmed asparagus, cut into
  short lengths
2½ cups baby spinach, chopped
⅓ cup dry vermouth or white wine
2 tablespoons chopped parsley
1¼ cups freshly grated Parmesan
  cheese
salt and pepper

Serves **4**
Prep time **10 minutes**
Cooking time **20 minutes**

1 Place the stock in a saucepan on a low heat until it simmers gently.

2 Melt half of the butter with the oil in a heavy saucepan, add the garlic and onion, and sauté gently for 5 minutes.

3 Add the rice and stir well to coat each grain with the butter and oil. Add enough stock to just cover the rice and stir well. Simmer gently, stirring frequently.

4 When most of the liquid is absorbed, add more stock and stir well. Continue adding the stock in stages and stirring until it is absorbed. Add the vegetables and vermouth or wine with the final amount of stock, mix well, and cook for 2 minutes.

5 Remove the pan from the heat, season, and add the remaining butter, the parsley, and Parmesan. Mix well and serve at once.

AFFORDABILITY
2

## Keeping stock

Meat and chicken stock will keep in the refrigerator for up to four days. Vegetable stock can be stored for up to two days. Fish stock should be used within 24 hours. If you want to keep stock longer freeze it in small containers.

# BASIL &
## TOMATO STEW

AFFORDABILITY
**1**

2 lb ripe tomatoes, skinned
¼ cup plus 2 tablespoons olive oil
2 onions, chopped
4 celery sticks, sliced
4 plump garlic cloves, thinly sliced
2¼ cups sliced mushrooms
3 tablespoons sun-dried tomato paste
2½ cups Vegetable Stock (see page 235)
1 tablespoon light brown sugar
3 tablespoons capers
large handful of basil leaves,
large handful of chervil or flat leaf parsley, about ½ oz
salt and pepper
warm bread, to serve

Serves **4**
Prep time **10 minutes**
Cooking time **15 minutes**

1 Quarter and seed the tomatoes, scooping out the pulp into a sieve over a bowl to catch the juices.

2 Heat ¼ cup oil in a large saucepan and fry the onions and celery for 5 minutes. Add the garlic and mushrooms and fry for an additional 3 minutes.

3 Add the tomatoes and their juices, the sun-dried tomato paste, stock, sugar, and capers and bring to a boil. Reduce the heat and simmer gently, uncovered, for 5 minutes.

4 Tear the herbs into pieces, add to the pan with a little salt and pepper and cook for 1 minute. Ladle into bowls, drizzle with the remaining oil, and serve with warm bread.

### Peeling garlic

A quick way to prepare garlic is to squash the bulb swiftly with the flat of your hand or under the flat blade of a large knife. The skin will come away easily, and you can chop, crush or add the whole clove to your dish, according to the recipe.

# BUTTERED CAULIFLOWER CRUMBLE

1 Cut the cauliflower into large florets and blanch in boiling water for 2 minutes. Drain the florets thoroughly.

2 Melt half the butter in a large skillet, add the bread crumbs, and fry for 2 minutes until golden. Drain and set aside.

3 Melt the remaining butter in the pan with the oil, add the cauliflower florets, and fry gently for about 5 minutes until golden. Add the capers, gherkins, dill or tarragon, and sour cream, season to taste with salt and pepper, and stir the mixture over a moderate heat for 1 minute.

4 Turn into a shallow flameproof dish and sprinkle with the fried bread crumbs and Parmesan. Cook under a preheated moderate broiler for about 2 minutes until the crumbs are dark golden brown.

1 large cauliflower
2 tablespoons butter
1 cup fresh bread crumbs
2 tablespoons olive oil
3 tablespoons capers
3 cocktail gherkins, finely chopped
3 tablespoons chopped dill or tarragon
scant ½ cup sour cream
¼ grated Parmesan cheese
salt and pepper

Serves **4**
Prep time **8 minutes**
Cooking time **12 minutes**

# OUTDOOR GRUB

GREEK-STYLE FETA SALAD

VEGETABLE KEBABS WITH PILAF

COLESLAW

BAKED TORTILLAS WITH HUMMUS

# LEMON & HERB BARBECUED CHICKEN WINGS

AFFORDABILITY
2

2 garlic cloves, crushed
grated zest and juice of
  1 lemon
4 thyme sprigs
¼ cup plus 2 tablespoons extra
  virgin olive oil
1 tablespoon honey
1 teaspoon dried oregano
1 teaspoon ground cumin
12 chicken wings
salt and pepper

Serves 4
Prep time **5 minutes**
Cooking time **15-20 minutes**

1 Put the garlic, lemon zest, and juice in a bowl, add the thyme, oil, honey, oregano, and cumin and season to taste with salt and pepper. Add the chicken wings and stir until well coated.

2 Barbecue or broil the chicken wings for 15-20 minutes, turning and basting until charred and cooked through.

## Barbecue basics

Barbecuing is a skill that needs to be mastered. The main issue is impatience — if you're cooking on coals, give them time to get really hot because they're not ready for food until the flames are out and they're glowing red. Remember, too, that a blackened burger doesn't necessarily mean a cooked burger — always check the food is cooked through before you potentially poison your mates.

# GREEN **CHICKEN** *KEBABS*

FRAGRANT AND BURSTING WITH FLAVOR, THESE
SUCCULENT CHICKEN SKEWERS ARE LOW IN FAT AND
MAKE AN EXCELLENT DISH WHEN SERVED WITH A
CRISP CUCUMBER AND RED ONION SALAD.

**1** Put the yogurt, garlic, ginger, cumin, ground coriander,
chile, chopped herbs, and lime juice in a blender and whiz
until fairly smooth. Season lightly.

**2** Cut the chicken into bite-size pieces and place in a large
mixing bowl. Pour over the spice mixture and toss to coat
evenly. Cover with plastic wrap and marinate in the refrigerator
for 4–6 hours or overnight if time permits.

**3** When ready to cook thread the chicken pieces onto eight
presoaked bamboo skewers. Barbecue for 8–10 minutes,
turning frequently, until cooked through and lightly browned.
Serve immediately with halves of lime to squeeze over.

scant ½ cup low-fat plain
    yogurt
2 garlic cloves, crushed
2 teaspoons finely grated
    fresh ginger root
2 teaspoons ground cumin
1 teaspoon ground
    coriander
1 green chile, finely chopped
large handful of chopped
    cilantro leaves
small handful of chopped
    mint leaves
juice of 2 limes
sea salt
4 boneless, skinless chicken
    breasts
halves of lime, to serve

Serves 4
Prep time **10 minutes, plus
marinating**
Cooking time **15 minutes**

AFFORDABILITY
2

# MINTED **LAMB** KEBABS

IF YOU'RE COOKING THESE ON A BARBECUE MAKE SURE THEY CHILL FOR PLENTY OF TIME TO ENSURE THEY STAY FIRM ON THE GRILL AND DON'T FALL APART.

1 tablespoon chickpea flour (besan or gram flour)
1¼ lb finely ground lamb
¼ cup plus 1 tablespoon finely chopped mint leaves
3 tablespoons finely chopped cilantro leaves
2 green chiles, seeded and finely chopped
2 teaspoons ground cumin
1 teaspoon ground coriander
½ medium egg, lightly beaten
sunflower oil, to brush
salt and pepper

Serves 4
Prep time **15 minutes, plus marinating**
Cooking time **12–15 minutes**

1 Put the flour, ground lamb, chopped mint and cilantro leaves, chiles, and the ground spices in a mixing bowl. Season, add the egg and, using your hands, mix until well combined. Cover and chill for 2–3 hours or overnight.

2 Line a large baking sheet with nonstick parchment paper. Shape the mixture into 12 balls, flatten slightly, and place on the baking sheet. Brush lightly with the oil and bake in a preheated oven, 375° F, for 12–15 minutes until cooked through. Remove, thread onto skewers, and serve immediately. Alternatively, you can cook the lamb balls over a barbecue, turning occasionally until they are cooked through.

AFFORDABILITY
2

## Wooden skewers

If you're barbecuing or broiling with wooden skewers, soak them in water for about half an hour before it's time to cook. While you expect the odd sausage to succumb to the flames on a barbecue, there's no joy to be had in watching the skewers catch light.

# *Shish* KEBABS

1 Mix all the ingredients, except the oil, in a large bowl until smooth. Divide the mixture into six equal-size, sausage-shaped patties.

2 Make the marinade. Mix together the yogurt, curry powder, and garlic in a flat-based dish. Thread the patties onto oiled metal skewers, immerse in the marinade, and leave for 2–4 hours.

3 Remove the skewers from the marinade. Brush the patties with oil and cook, turning occasionally, on a medium-hot barbecue for 10–15 minutes.

4 Serve hot with the onion, bell pepper, and parsley, dusted over with paprika, and with lemon wedges to squeeze over.

12 oz ground lamb
1 onion, finely chopped
2 teaspoons lemon juice
1 egg, beaten
2 tablespoons all-purpose flour
2 tablespoons chopped cilantro
½ teaspoon salt
oil, for brushing

**Marinade**
¼ cup plain yogurt
1 tablespoon medium or hot
   curry powder
1 garlic clove, crushed

**To serve**
red onion, finely sliced
red bell pepper, finely sliced
1 tablespoon chopped parsley
1 teaspoon paprika
lemon wedges

Serves **6**
Prep time **15 minutes, plus marinating**
Cooking time **10–15 minutes**

AFFORDABILITY

# SPICY MAPLE RIBS

THESE ARE GREAT FOR SUMMER PARTIES AND CAN BE PACKED UP AND TAKEN ON A PICNIC. REMEMBER TO BASTE SEVERAL TIMES DURING COOKING TO MAKE THE MOST OF THEIR DELICIOUSLY DARK, STICKY GLAZE.

2½ lb meaty pork spare ribs
scant ½ cup maple syrup
2 garlic cloves, crushed
3 tablespoons white wine vinegar
3 tablespoons tomato paste
finely grated zest and juice of 1 lemon
1 red chile, seeded and finely chopped
½ teaspoon smoked paprika
salt
lemon or lime halves, to serve

Serves **4**
Prep time **10 minutes, plus marinating**
Cooking time 1½-1¾ **hours**

1 Arrange the meat in a single layer in a shallow, nonmetallic dish. Mix together the maple syrup, garlic, vinegar, tomato paste, lemon zest and juice, chile and paprika. Pour the mixture over the ribs, turning them until they are completely coated, cover, and marinate in the refrigerator for 4-24 hours.

2 Transfer the ribs to a shallow roasting pan and pour over the excess marinade from the dish. Season lightly with salt and bake in a preheated oven, 350°F, for 1½-1¾ hours, basting occasionally with the juices, until the meat is tender and the juices are thick and sticky.

3 Transfer to serving plates and serve immediately with lemon or lime halves for squeezing over.

AFFORDABILITY 2

# MUSTARD-GRILLED
## Sardines

THESE DELICIOUSLY SPICY SARDINES ARE GREAT
SERVED SIMPLY WITH A FRESH, CRUNCHY SALAD AND
LEMON WEDGES FOR SQUEEZING OVER.

12 sardines
1 tablespoon whole-grain
  mustard
juice of 2 lemons
1 teaspoon chili powder
1 teaspoon garam masala
salt and pepper
lemon wedges, to serve

**Serves 4**
**Prep time 10 minutes**
**Cooking time 6-8 minutes**

**1** Put the sardines on a large work surface and use a sharp knife to make two or three diagonal slashes on both sides of each fish.

**2** In a small bowl mix together the mustard, lemon juice, chili powder, and garam masala. Season to taste and spread this mixture over the fish.

**3** Cook on a medium-hot barbecue for 3-4 minutes on each side or until cooked through. Serve hot with wedges of lemon.

# SALMON WITH FENNEL
## *& Tomatoes*

*FISH IS A FANTASTIC AND REFRESHING SUMMER SUPPER. THESE CAN BE EASILY BARBECUED BY WRAPPING THE FILLETS IN FOIL AFTER COATING.*

**1** Season the salmon fillets generously with salt and pepper and pour over the lemon juice. Set aside.

**2** In a small bowl mix together the oil, vinegar, honey, garlic. Season to taste with salt and pepper. Put the onions, fennel, and tomatoes in a large bowl and pour over the oil mixture. Toss to coat thoroughly, then spread out on a baking sheet.

**3** Roast in a preheated oven, 425ºF, for 10 minutes. Add the salmon fillets to the baking sheet and roast for an additional 12-15 minutes. Serve the salmon with the roasted vegetables and rice or couscous.

4 salmon fillets, 6-8 oz each
¼ cup lemon juice
¼ cup olive oil
1 tablespoon balsamic vinegar
1 tablespoon honey
4 garlic cloves, finely chopped
2 red onions, quartered
2 fennel bulbs, quartered
16-20 vine cherry tomatoes
salt and pepper
rice or couscous, to serve

**Serves 4**
**Prep time 10 minutes**
**Cooking time 22-25 minutes**

AFFORDABILITY
**3**

# FEEL THE
# BURN

### BEFORE YOU START

Rub a bit of oil over the grill rack before you start to cook. This helps to prevent the food from sticking to the rack.

### SAFETY FIRST

Make sure the barbecue is completely cold before you leave it—a stray spark could mean a frantic call to the fire service later on.

### THE ART OF BARBECUE

It's unlikely that you will be able to afford a swish barbecue, which means you're going to have to take your chances with charcoal in a tin tub on wobbly legs. If the food's cooked well, it doesn't matter if you procured your cooking vessel on a late-night drunken dumpster raid, but there are certain rules that need to be followed if you don't want to poison your mates, don't want to lose your facial hair, and don't want your burgers to taste (and look) as if they've been excavated from an archaeological dig.

Like any other cooking method, barbecuing is an art, and there's a lot of multitasking involved. You have to appear as though you're casually flipping sausages over hot coals, but at the same time you need to swap jokes with your mates and take regular gulps from a can of lager. Get your timings wrong and you could either run out of beer or overcook a sausage. Here are a few tips that should see you wallowing in a sea of praise.

## TAKE YOUR TIME

Exercise a little patience, the secret weapon of the successful barbecue chef. It's always tempting to start cooking the meat before the coals are hot enough, but you should aim to light the coals at least 30 minutes before you cook, which is how long it takes for the flames to die down and the charcoal to be burning hot.

## COOK YOUR MEAT THOROUGHLY

If you're worried about cooking times (or just cooking the meat properly), cut larger pieces of meat or burgers in half lengthwise.

## BIG PARTY?

If you have a small barbecue and a large number of guests, crank up the oven and transfer cooked food to keep it warm while you finish off on the barbie.

## SIMPLICITY RULES

Keep it simple. Don't be too ambitious with the food. It's far better to stick to a couple of meat choices, something for veggies and a few simple side dishes. This isn't a gourmet dinner party; it's cooking over fire.

# CHEESE & SPINACH *Tart*

4 tablespoons butter
1 small onion, finely chopped
1 garlic clove, crushed
2 teaspoons chopped thyme
8 oz frozen leaf spinach
  (thawed)
¾ cup light cream
2 eggs, beaten
¼ cup grated Parmesan cheese
8-inch frozen pie crust (cook
  from frozen)
salt and black pepper
green salad, to serve

1 Melt the butter in a large skillet, add the onion, garlic, thyme, and salt and pepper to taste and cook for 5 minutes. Squeeze out all the excess water from the spinach, add to the pan and cook, stirring, for 2–3 minutes until heated through.

2 In a bowl beat together the cream, eggs, cheese, and a pinch of salt and pepper. Spoon the spinach mixture into the tart shell, carefully pour over the cream mixture, and bake on a preheated baking sheet in a preheated oven, 400°F, for 20 minutes until set. Serve with a green salad.

Serves **4**
Prep time **10 minutes**
Cooking time **25 minutes**

# MUSTARD & THYME
## SWEET POTATOES

1 Wrap each potato in a double layer of kitchen foil and either place them on the flat plate of a gas barbecue or, using barbecue tongs, set them in among the heated coals of a charcoal barbecue, allowing some of the coals to cover the potatoes. Bake for 40 minutes.

2 Meanwhile, make the butter. Put the butter, mustard, thyme, and some pepper in a bowl and mash with a fork until evenly mixed. Set aside.

3 Remove the potatoes from the barbecue (again using tongs) and carefully remove the foil using oven mitts. Cut the potatoes in half and serve topped with the butter.

6 sweet potatoes, about 8 oz each, scrubbed

**Mustard and thyme butter**
¼ lb (1 stick) butter, softened
1 tablespoon whole-grain mustard
1 teaspoon chopped thyme
pepper

Serves **6**
Prep time **5 minutes**
Cooking time **40 minutes**

AFFORDABILITY
1

# Barbecued CORN
## WITH CHILI & LIME

CHARGRILLING CORN GIVES IT A SMOKY FLAVOR, WHICH IS SET OFF BY THE SPICY CHILI AND SHARP, TANGY LIME JUICE.

4 ears of corn
1 tablespoon coarse chili powder
1 tablespoon sea salt
2 limes, halved

Serves **4**
Prep time **5 minutes**
Cooking time **8-10 minutes**

 **1** Neatly remove the husks from the corn and reserve to serve the final dish on.

**2** Mix together the chili powder and sea salt and put on a small plate or saucer.

**3** Cook the corn over a medium heat over a barbecue or under a medium-hot broiler for 4-5 minutes, turning them around so that they cook all over, until the corn is lightly charred in places. Remove from the heat, dip a lime half in the chili mixture and squeeze and spread it over the corn to coat evenly. Repeat with the remaining corn and lime and chili mixture. Set the corn on the reserved husks and eat immediately.

# GUACAMOLE
# WITH TOTOPOS

THIS DELICIOUS DIP IS PREPARED ALL OVER ITS NATIVE MEXICO AND CAN
BE SERVED AS A SIDE DISH TO GRILLED MEATS, SALADS, AND RICE OR SIMPLY
SPOONED OVER ANY KIND OF TACO.

2 large ripe avocados
1 tablespoon finely chopped
 onion
2 serrano or jalapeño chiles,
 finely chopped
2 tablespoons finely chopped
 cilantro, plus extra leaves to
 garnish
squeeze of lime juice
salt

**Totopos**
soft corn tortillas
vegetable oil, for brushing

Serves **4**
Prep time **15 minutes**
Cooking time **8-10 minutes**

1 Make the totopos. Brush each side of the tortillas with a little oil and cut into triangles. Arrange on a baking sheet and bake in a preheated oven, 350°F, for 8-10 minutes until crisp. Sprinkle with a little salt and allow to cool on a wire rack.

2 Halve the avocados and remove the pits. Cut the flesh into ½-inch cubes, then use a spoon to scoop out the remaining flesh from the skin and put it in a bowl.

3 Add the onion, chiles, and cilantro to the bowl and mix together gently, without squashing the avocado. Add a little lime juice to taste and season to taste with salt. Garnish with cilantro leaves and serve immediately with the totopos.

# VEGETABLE KEBABS WITH PILAF

1 In a large bowl combine the rosemary with 2 tablespoons oil and salt and pepper. Cut the zucchini and bell pepper into large pieces, add to the oil with the mushrooms and tomatoes, and toss well. Cover and allow to marinate for 20 minutes.

2 Wash the rice under cold water, drain, and put in a saucepan. Add lightly salted water to cover the rice by at least 2 inches. Bring to a boil and boil for 10 minutes. Drain well.

3 Heat the remaining oil in a separate saucepan, add the onion, garlic, and cardamom pods and cook over a medium heat, stirring frequently, for 5 minutes until lightly golden. Add the rice, cranberries, pistachios, and cilantro. Season to taste with salt and pepper. Stir well, remove from the heat, cover and allow to rest for 10 minutes.

4 Meanwhile, thread the vegetables alternately onto eight presoaked wooden skewers. Cook on a medium-hot barbecue, turning frequently, for 10 minutes until all the vegetables are tender. Serve with the rice and Greek-style yogurt.

1 tablespoon chopped rosemary
¼ cup plus 1 tablespoon extra virgin olive oil
2 zucchini
1 large red bell pepper, cored and seeded
16 white mushrooms, trimmed
8 cherry tomatoes
Greek-style yogurt, to serve

**Pilaf**
1¼ cups basmati rice
1 onion, finely chopped
2 garlic cloves, finely chopped
6 cardamom pods, bruised
¾ cup dried cranberries
½ cup pistachios, toasted and chopped
2 tablespoons chopped cilantro
salt and pepper

Serves **4**
Prep time **20 minutes, plus marinating and resting**
Cooking time **20 minutes**

# NASI GORENG

A QUICK AND TASTY SUMMER SUPPER TO ENJOY
IN THE SUN AND REMIND YOU OF YOUR GAP YEAR
TREKKING ACROSS INDONESIA.

1 Heat the oil in a wok or large skillet, add the chicken, and
stir-fry for 1 minute. Add the shrimp, garlic, carrot, and
cabbage and stir-fry for 3–4 minutes.

2 Pour in the egg and spread it with a wooden spoon. Cook
until set, then break it up. Add the rice and stir to mix.

3 Add the soy sauce, sesame oil, and chili sauce and heat
through. Serve immediately, garnished with chile strips.

2 tablespoons vegetable oil
5 oz boneless, skinless chicken
breast, finely chopped
2 oz cooked peeled shrimp
(thawed if frozen)
1 garlic clove, crushed
1 carrot, shredded
¼ white cabbage, thinly sliced
1 egg, beaten
2¼ cups cold cooked basmati
rice
2 tablespoons sweet soy sauce
(kecap manis)
½ teaspoon sesame oil
1 tablespoon chili sauce
1 red chile, seeded and cut into
strips, to garnish

Serves 4
Prep time 10 minutes
Cooking time 10 minutes

AFFORDABILITY
3

# CHEESY GARLIC BREAD

1   Cut 20 slices in the baguette without going all the way through. Combine the oil, garlic, thyme, and salt and pepper in a bowl and brush the mixture all over the cut sides and the top of the bread.

2   Put a slice of mozzarella between each slice of bread, place the loaf on a double layer of kitchen foil and seal loosely. Cook on a medium-hot barbecue for 5 minutes, then open out the foil (using oven mitts because the foil will be hot) and cook for 5 minutes more. Serve hot.

1 small French baguette
⅓ cup extra virgin olive oil
1 garlic clove, crushed
2 teaspoons chopped thyme
4 oz buffalo mozzarella cheese, thinly sliced
salt and black pepper

Serves 4
Prep time **5 minutes**
Cooking time **10 minutes**

# CAESAR SALAD

1 garlic clove, crushed
4 anchovy fillets, chopped
¼ cup lemon juice
2 teaspoons powdered English mustard
1 egg yolk
scant 1 cup extra virgin olive oil
vegetable oil, for frying
3 slices of country bread, cubed
1 romaine lettuce, washed and torn into pieces
3 tablespoons grated Parmesan cheese
pepper

Serves 4
Prep time **20 minutes**
Cooking time **5 minutes**

1 Put the garlic, anchovy fillets, lemon juice, mustard, and egg yolk in a small mixing bowl and season with pepper. Use an electric hand blender or small whisk to mix well until combined. Drizzle in the olive oil, mixing all the time, to make a thick, creamy sauce. If the sauce becomes too thick, add a little water.

2 Heat the vegetable oil in a skillet. Test with a small piece of bread to see if it is hot enough; if the bread sizzles, add the bread cubes, turning them when they are golden. When they are cooked, transfer them to a plate lined with paper towels to absorb the excess oil.

3 Put the lettuce in a large bowl, pour over the dressing and 2 tablespoons grated Parmesan and mix well.

4 Serve the salad in a large bowl or on individual plates, sprinkled with the croutons and the remaining Parmesan.

# TOMATO & GREEN BEAN SALAD

1 Cut the tomatoes into halves and put them into a large bowl.

2 Cook the green beans in boiling water for 2 minutes, drain well, and place in the bowl with the tomatoes.

3 Add the mint, garlic, oil, and vinegar. Season to taste with salt and pepper and mix well. Serve warm or cold.

1 cup baby red tomatoes (plum if possible)
2 cups thin green beans, topped and tailed
handful of mint, chopped
1 garlic clove, crushed and chopped
¼ cup extra virgin olive oil
1 tablespoon balsamic vinegar
salt and pepper

Serves **4**
Prep time **10 minutes**
Cooking time **2 minutes**

# GREEK-STYLE
# FETA
# SALAD

4 tomatoes, cut into wedges
½ cucumber, cut into bite-size
  cubes
1 red bell pepper, cored, seeded,
  and cut into rings or thinly
  sliced
1 red onion, thinly sliced
7 oz feta cheese, cubed
½ cup pitted black olives
¼ cup olive oil
2 tablespoons white wine
  vinegar
2-3 teaspoons finely chopped
  oregano
salt and pepper

Serves **4**
Prep time **15 minutes**

1 Arrange the tomatoes, cucumber, bell pepper, and onion in a
serving dish.

2 Sprinkle the cheese and olives over the salad, season well
with salt and pepper, and drizzle with the oil and vinegar.
Sprinkle over the oregano before serving.

# COLESLAW

½ white cabbage
¼ red cabbage
2 carrots
1 red onion
2 tablespoons coarsely chopped
    parsley

**Dressing**
1¼ cups mayonnaise
1 tablespoon white wine vinegar
½ teaspoon sugar
salt and pepper

Serves **4**
Prep time **15 minutes, plus
standing**

1 Finely shred both cabbages and the carrots and finely slice
the onion. Mix the cabbages and carrots in a large salad
bowl with the onion and add the parsley.

2 Make the dressing by whisking together the mayonnaise,
vinegar, and sugar. Season to taste with salt and pepper.
Toss the dressing through the cabbage mixture, then allow to
stand for at least 30 minutes before serving.

AFFORDABILITY
1

# POTATO SALAD

**AFFORDABILITY**

1 Halve the potatoes and cook in lightly salted boiling water until tender. Rinse under cold water and allow to cool.

2 Meanwhile, cut the bacon into thin strips. Heat the oil in a skillet, add the bacon, and cook until golden. Drain on paper towels and allow to cool. Finely slice the green onions, reserving some for garnish.

3 Put the potatoes, finely sliced green onions, and bacon in a large salad bowl. Gently stir in the mayonnaise. Season to taste with salt and pepper, garnish with the reserved green onions, and serve.

2 lb new potatoes
4 oz smoked bacon
1 teaspoon vegetable oil
6 green onions
¾ cup mayonnaise
salt and pepper

Serves **4-6**
Prep time **10 minutes, plus cooling**
Cooking time **15 minutes**

# PANZANELLA

3 red bell peppers, cored,
seeded, and quartered
12 oz ripe plum tomatoes,
skinned
¼ cup plus 2 tablespoons extra
virgin olive oil
3 tablespoons wine vinegar
2 garlic cloves, crushed
4 oz stale ciabatta bread (about
4 slices)
⅓ cup pitted black olives
small handful of basil leaves,
shredded
salt and pepper

Serves 4
Prep time **15 minutes**
Cooking time **10 minutes**

**1** Put the peppers, skin side up, on a foil-lined broiler rack and broil under a preheated moderate broiler for 10 minutes or until the skins are blackened.

**2** Meanwhile, quarter the tomatoes and scoop out the pulp, placing it in a sieve over a bowl to catch the juices. Set the tomato quarters aside. Press the pulp with the back of a spoon to extract as much juice as possible. Beat the oil, vinegar, garlic, and salt and pepper into the tomato juice.

**3** When they are cool enough to handle, peel the skins from the peppers and discard. Roughly slice the peppers and place in a bowl with the tomato quarters. Break the bread into small chunks and add to the bowl with the olives and basil.

**4**  Add the dressing and toss the ingredients together before serving.

# WARM **ZUCCHINI** *&* **LIME** SALAD

IF YOU PREFER, YOU CAN COOK THIN SLICES OF
EGGPLANT IN THE SAME WAY.

**1** Put the oil, lime zest and juice, garlic, cilantro and a little salt and pepper in a plastic bag. Add the zucchini and shake gently in the bag to coat. Seal and set aside until ready to cook.

**2** Heat a ridged grill pan until smoking. Arrange as many zucchini slices as will fit in a single layer over the base of the pan and cook for 2–3 minutes until the undersides are browned. Turn the zucchini over and brown on the other side, then transfer to a warmed serving dish while you cook the remainder.

**3** Pour any remaining dressing over the zucchini, sprinkle with chopped cilantro to garnish and serve immediately.

1 tablespoon olive oil
finely grated zest and juice of
  1 lime
1 garlic clove, finely chopped
2 tablespoons roughly
  chopped cilantro leaves,
  plus extra to garnish
2 zucchini, about 11 oz in
  total, cut into thin diagonal
  slices
salt and pepper

**Serves 4**
**Prep time 10 minutes**
**Cooking time 8 minutes**

4 small wheat tortillas
1 tablespoon olive oil

**Hummus**
1 13-oz can chickpeas, rinsed
  and drained
1 garlic clove, chopped
4-6 tablespoons plain yogurt
2 tablespoons lemon juice
1 tablespoon chopped cilantro
  leaves
salt and pepper
paprika, to sprinkle

**To serve**
lemon wedges
olives

Serves 4
Prep time **5 minutes**
Cooking time **10-12 minutes**

# BAKED
# TORTILLAS
## *WITH* HUMMUS

1 Cut each tortilla into 8 triangles, put them on a baking sheet
  and brush with a little oil. Cook in a preheated oven, 400°F,
for 10-12 minutes, until golden and crisp. Remove from the oven.

2 Meanwhile, put the chickpeas, garlic, yogurt, and lemon
  juice in a bowl and mix thoroughly until smooth. Sprinkle
with salt and pepper, stir in the cilantro, and sprinkle with
paprika. Serve with the warm tortillas, lemon wedges, and olives.

# FALAFEL cakes

*AFFORDABILITY* **1**

AS WELL AS MAKING A TASTY, HEALTHY DINNER, THESE ARE A GREAT ADDITION TO ANY PICNIC WHEN SERVED WITH HUMMUS (SEE OPPOSITE).

**1** Put the chickpeas in a food processor or blender with the onion, garlic, spices, herbs, bread crumbs, and a little salt and pepper. Blend briefly to make a chunky paste.

**2** Take dessertspoonfuls of the mixture and flatten into cakes. Add oil to a skillet to a depth of ½ inch, heat, and fry half the falafel for about 3 minutes, turning once, until crisp and golden. Drain on paper towels and keep warm while you cook the remainder.

1 13-oz can chickpeas, rinsed and drained
1 onion, coarsely chopped
3 garlic cloves, coarsely chopped
2 teaspoons cumin seeds
1 teaspoon mild chili powder
2 tablespoons chopped mint
3 tablespoons chopped cilantro
1 cup fresh bread crumbs
oil, for pan-frying
salt and pepper

Serves **4**
Prep time **10 minutes**
Cooking time **10 minutes**

# ORANGE SUPER-SMOOTHIE

1 large carrot
1 orange
1 banana
1 fresh or dried apricot
2-3 ice cubes

1 Peel the carrot and orange and juice the two together. If you are using a blender, chop into smaller pieces.

2 Transfer the juice to a food processor or blender, add the banana, apricot, and a couple of ice cubes. Blend briefly.

3 Pour the smoothie into a glass and serve immediately.

Serves **1**
Prep time **5 minutes**

AFFORDABILITY
**1**

# BANANA *&* PEANUT BUTTER SMOOTHIE

*THIS IS TASTY ENOUGH TO SATISFY EVERYONE'S SWEET CRAVINGS (AND SAVE YOU THE LONG QUEUES AT THE ICE CREAM VAN).*

1 ripe banana
1¼ cups low-fat milk
1 tablespoon smooth peanut
    butter or 2 teaspoons tahini
    paste

1 Peel and slice the banana, put it in a freezer container, and freeze for at least 2 hours or overnight.

2 Put the banana, milk, and peanut butter or tahini paste in a food processor or blender and process until smooth.

3 Pour the smoothie into 2 tall glasses. Serve immediately.

Serves **2**
Prep time **5 minutes, plus freezing**

AFFORDABILITY
**1**

AFFORDABILITY
1

# STRAWBERRY LASSI

REFRESHING AND PACKED WITH VITAMIN C, THIS MAKES A GREAT
ALTERNATIVE TO DRINKING BEERS ALL DAY IN THE PARK.

1 Put the strawberries in a food processor with half the cold water. Blend until smooth.

2 Add the yogurt, sugar, remaining water, and the rose water and blitz until smooth and frothy. Pour into chilled, tall glasses, sprinkle with black pepper, and serve immediately.

2²/₃ cups strawberries, hulled
   and roughly chopped
3 cups ice cold water
1¼ cups low-fat plain yogurt
2 tablespoons unrefined sugar
few drops of rose water
coarsely ground black pepper,
   to serve

Serves **4**
Prep time **10 minutes**

GRILLED VEGETABLE
& HALOUMI SALAD

PESTO ALLA GENOVESE

# **FRIENDS**
# FOR DINNER

TURKEY WITH CREOLE SAUCE

# CHICKEN FAJITAS

1 tablespoon olive oil
1 large red onion, thinly sliced
1 red bell pepper, cored, seeded, and thinly sliced
1 yellow bell pepper, cored, seeded, and thinly sliced
14½ oz boneless, skinless chicken breasts, cut into thin strips
⅛ teaspoon paprika
⅛ teaspoon mild chili powder
⅛ teaspoon ground cumin
¼ teaspoon dried oregano
4 soft flour tortillas
½ iceberg lettuce, finely shredded
guacamole, to serve (optional)

**Tomato salsa**

1 small red onion, finely chopped
14 oz small vine-ripened tomatoes, chopped
2 garlic cloves, crushed
large handful of cilantro leaves, chopped
pepper

Serves **4**
Prep time **15 minutes, plus chilling**
Cooking time **10 minutes**

1 To prepare the tomato salsa, in a small bowl mix together the chopped onion, tomatoes, garlic, and cilantro. Season with pepper, cover, and chill for 30 minutes to allow the flavors to develop.

2 Heat the oil in a wok or large, nonstick skillet, add the onion and peppers and cook for 3–4 minutes. Add the chicken, paprika, chili powder, cumin, and oregano and stir-fry for 5 minutes until the chicken is cooked through.

3 Meanwhile, wrap the tortillas in kitchen foil and warm them in the oven for 5 minutes or according to the package directions.

4 Spoon one-quarter of the chicken mixture into the center of each tortilla and add a couple of tablespoons of the salsa and some shredded lettuce. Roll up and serve warm, accompanied by guacamole, if desired.

## Chops away

For the price of a round of happy-hour drinks, you can invest in a mini food processor. They make short work of chopping onions, garlic, chiles, and other ingredients, saving you valuable drinking time and avoiding close contact with sharp knives.

AFFORDABILITY
2

# SPANISH MARINADE
## WITH CHICKEN

1 Make the marinade. Mix together all the ingredients and season to taste with salt and pepper. Rub the marinade thoroughly into the skin of the chicken. Drizzle the olive oil over the chicken and allow to marinate in the refrigerator for at least 2 hours, but preferably overnight.

2 Transfer the chicken to a roasting pan and cook in a preheated oven, 350°F, for 1½ hours.

3 Put the chicken on a warm plate, cover with kitchen foil, and allow to rest in a warm place for about 10 minutes before carving.

1 large chicken, about 4 lb
¼ cup Spanish extra virgin olive oil

**Marinade**
1 cup full-fat plain yogurt
1 teaspoon smoked paprika
grated zest and juice of 1 lemon
1 tablespoon red wine vinegar
1 small onion, finely grated
2 garlic cloves, crushed
2 tablespoons chopped parsley, plus extra for serving
salt and pepper

Serves **4**
Prep time **12 minutes, plus marinating and resting**
Cooking time 1½ **hours**

# SUCCULENT
# ROAST CHICKEN

5 oz soft goat cheese
1 hot red chile, seeded and
  chopped
1 oz prosciutto, chopped
3 garlic cloves, crushed
2 teaspoons chopped
  rosemary, plus several extra
  sprigs
small handful flat leaf parsley,
  chopped
3-lb chicken
4 tablespoons butter, softened
1 large glass of white wine
salt

Serves **5-6**
Prep time **20 minutes**
Cooking time **1½ hours**

*PACKING STUFFING UNDER THE SKIN OF A CHICKEN IS THE BEST WAY TO LET THE DELICIOUS FLAVORS PENETRATE THE MEAT. IT ALSO SEEPS RIGHT THROUGH TO THE JUICES FOR THE GRAVY.*

1 Mix together the cheese, chile, prosciutto, garlic, chopped rosemary, parsley, and a little salt.

2 Slide your fingers between the chicken breast and skin, then push a little further under the skin to release the skin from the tops of the leg joints. Use a teaspoon to pack the cheese mixture between the skin and the meat. Smooth the skin back into place, at the same time spreading the stuffing in an even layer.

3 So that the chicken keeps its shape during cooking it's usual to truss the bird before cooking it. Take a long piece of butcher's twine and put the chicken on a board with the legs toward you. Center the twine under the legs, pass it over the legs, and pull the ends so that the legs cross and are held securely together. Wind the ends once round the legs and then take them down the sides so that the wings are pressed against the body. Turn over the bird and make sure the flap of skin at the neck end is tucked neatly into the aperture. Fasten the twine in a bow (for easy removal).

4 Sit the chicken over the extra rosemary sprigs in a roasting pan and spread with the butter. Roast in a preheated oven, 375°F, for 1½ hours or until the juices run clear when the thigh is pierced with a skewer.

5 Drain to a serving plate and allow to stand in a warm place for 15 minutes. Add the wine to the roasting pan, stirring to scrape up the residue, and allow it to bubble for a few minutes. Check the seasoning and serve with the chicken.

## Jointing a chicken

It's cheaper to buy a whole chicken and joint it yourself than to buy separate portions. Using a really sharp knife, cut down the length of the back of the chicken, then open it out flat onto the cutting board and cut through the breast bone, so you now have two halves. Cut along the natural line of skin to separate the legs from the breasts and cut the legs from the thighs if you need six portions. Easy!

# BAKED **TURKEY** BURRITO

¼ cup vegetable oil
1 lb turkey breast, thinly sliced
1 large onion, sliced
1 red bell pepper, cored, seeded,
    and sliced
1 yellow bell pepper, cored, seeded,
    and sliced
1 5-oz can red kidney beans, rinsed
    and drained
1 cup cooked rice
juice of 1 lime
8 plain flour tortillas
¼ cup plus 2 tablespoons medium-
    hot salsa
2 tablespoons sliced preserved
    jalapeño chiles (optional)
2¼ cups grated cheddar cheese
salt and pepper

**To serve**
guacamole
½ iceberg lettuce, shredded

Serves **4**
Prep time **12 minutes**
Cooking time **30-33 minutes**

1 Heat 2 tablespoons oil in a large skillet and stir-fry the sliced turkey for 3-4 minutes until it is beginning to color. Remove it with a slotted spoon. Increase the heat, add the remaining oil, and fry the onion and peppers for 5-6 minutes, stirring only occasionally so that they color quickly without softening too much.

2 Reduce the heat, return the turkey to the pan, and stir in the beans and cooked rice. Season well, squeeze over the lime juice, and remove from the heat. Spoon the filling onto the tortillas, roll them up and arrange them in a single layer in a rectangular heatproof dish.

3 Pour the salsa over the tortillas and sprinkle with the jalapeño chiles (if used) and cheese. Cook in a preheated oven, 400°F, for about 20 minutes until hot and the cheese has melted. Serve immediately with guacamole and shredded lettuce.

# TURKEY WITH CREOLE SAUCE

FRYING TURKEY PIECES IN A CRISP, SPICY CRUMB COATING KEEPS THE MEAT MOIST AND SUCCULENT. THE PINEAPPLE AND PEPPER SAUCE ADDS A DELICIOUS CONTRAST IN BOTH TEXTURE AND FLAVOR.

**1** Cut the turkey across into ½-inch thick slices, then cut each slice into ½-inch strips. Mix the paprika, flour, and a little salt and coat the turkey in the mixture. Dip the turkey in the beaten egg and then in the bread crumbs until coated.

**2** Make the sauce. Heat the oil in a sauté pan or large skillet and gently fry the onion and peppers for 5–8 minutes until softened. Add the garlic, tomatoes, pineapple, Tabasco sauce, and a little salt to the pan and cook gently, stirring frequently, for about 10 minutes or until pulpy. If the pineapple isn't very sweet add a little sugar to the sauce.

**3** Heat ½ inch of oil in a pan until a few bread crumbs gently sizzle. Fry half the turkey pieces in the oil until golden, turning once. Drain on paper towels while you cook the rest. Serve with the sauce.

1 lb turkey breast fillet
½ teaspoon paprika
1 tablespoon all-purpose flour
1 egg, beaten
2 cups fresh bread crumbs
vegetable oil, for frying
salt

**Creole sauce**
2 tablespoons vegetable oil
1 onion, chopped
2 red bell peppers, cored, seeded, and chopped
2 garlic cloves, crushed
2½ cups skinned and chopped tomatoes (1 lb)
1 small, sweet pineapple, skinned, cored, and chopped
2 teaspoons Tabasco sauce

Serves **4**
Prep time **25 minutes**
Cooking time **25 minutes**

AFFORDABILITY 1

# CRISPY
## DUCK LEGS
## WITH MINI
## ROAST POTATOES

4 duck legs
1 tablespoon chopped thyme
2 teaspoons sea salt
½ teaspoon pepper
½ cup extra virgin olive oil
1 frisée lettuce

**Mini roast potatoes**
3 tablespoons extra virgin olive oil
2-3 thyme sprigs
1½ lb floury potatoes, cubed
4 garlic cloves
salt and pepper

**Dressing**
3 tablespoons extra virgin olive oil
1 tablespoon shallot vinegar
1 shallot, preferably purple, very
　finely diced
¼ teaspoon Dijon mustard
pinch of sugar

Serves **4**
Prep time **10 minutes, plus
marinating**
Cooking time **1½ hours**

*IN THIS MODERN TWIST ON THE CLASSIC ROAST, THE
CRISP SKIN OF THE POTATOES COMPLEMENTS THE
RICH DUCK MEAT, WHICH IS GENTLY FLAVORED BY
THE THYME.*

1 Rub the duck legs in the thyme, salt, and pepper, cover, and leave at room temperature for about 1 hour.

2 Heat the olive oil in a shallow flameproof casserole and place the duck legs, flesh side down, in the oil. Cook in a preheated oven, 375°F, for about 1½ hours, basting occasionally, until the flesh is tender.

3 Prepare the roast potatoes. Put the olive oil and thyme sprigs in a bowl and season well with salt and pepper. Add the potatoes and garlic and toss well. Tip them into a roasting pan and roast alongside the duck for about 45 minutes until they are golden and crispy.

4 Whisk together the dressing ingredients, toss with the lettuce to coat well with dressing, and serve with the crispy duck and potatoes.

# POT-ROASTED
## PORK *with*
## LENTILS

1 Cook the lentils in boiling water for 20 minutes. Drain and set aside.

2 Season the meat on all sides. Melt the butter with the oil in a large, heavy skillet and sear the meat on all sides until it is browned. Transfer the pork to a large casserole dish.

3 Add the onions to the pan and fry for 5 minutes. Add the garlic and rosemary sprigs and cook for 1 minute. Tip the onion and herbs into the casserole dish and cover with a lid. Roast in a preheated oven, 350°F, for 1¼ hours.

4 Tip the lentils around the meat and add the capers, anchovies, wine, and seasoning. Return to the oven for an additional 30 minutes, then allow to stand for 15 minutes before carving.

generous 1 cup Puy lentils, rinsed
3-lb pork loin roast, skinned, boned, and rolled
4 tablespoons butter
2 tablespoons olive oil
2 onions, sliced
4 garlic cloves, crushed
several rosemary sprigs
2 tablespoons capers, rinsed and drained
5 anchovy fillets, chopped
scant 1 cup white wine
salt and pepper

Serves **6**
Prep time **20 minutes, plus standing**
Cooking time **2 hours**

## Cooked meat

Don't let food poisoning add to the number of duvet days you take during term time. When it comes to cooking meat, you can't take any chances, so always follow the cooking instructions exactly. To make sure your meat is cooked through, push a skewer or sharp, thin-bladed knife into the thickest part—if the juices run clear, you're in the clear; if they're pink, the meat needs more cooking time.

# LET ME
## ENTERTAIN
# YOU

◇◇◇◇◇◇◇◇◇◇◇◇◇◇◇◇◇◇◇◇◇◇◇◇◇◇◇◇◇◇◇◇◇◇◇◇◇◇◇◇◇◇◇◇◇◇◇◇◇◇

If your idea of a dinner party is Chinese take-out and as many beers as you can carry, think again. With forward planning you can create an ambience and menu to mark you out as the "sophisticated student."

## PLAN AHEAD

Every good host(ess) will tell you that a successful dinner party relies almost entirely on good planning (burned food, power outages, or food poisoning could obviously put a bit of a damper on proceedings, but let's assume they're off the menu). It's true that you probably don't have the budget, time, or home entertaining skills (no offense) to throw a bash worthy of note in a food magazine, but if you plan ahead and make lots of lists there's less potential for disaster. Decide on your menu a week in advance to allow time to shop according to your means, and give people plenty of notice about the date—although this isn't quite as important as most students would miss the Second Coming for a free meal.

## FIGURE YOUR FLATWARE

There's nothing worse than being found wanting on the crockery and flatware front. Although you could substitute paper plates for porcelain at a push, no one wants to eat mashed potato or pasta with their fingers. Check you have enough knives, forks, plates, and glasses a day or two before and borrow extras if you need to.

## BRING A BOTTLE

It's all very well you making the effort to cook for your mates, but you shouldn't have to supply all the booze as well. Make it clear that your guests should bring a bottle of whatever they fancy drinking or you could be left hosting a dry dinner party. There are always a few who—if left unprompted—will arrive holding nothing more than their coat and spend the night drinking everyone else's alcohol.

## KEEP IT SIMPLE

Don't try to cook beyond your capabilities. Plan an easy menu that you know you can prepare without giving yourself a nervous breakdown. A simple, cold starter (such as Caesar Salad, page 60) is ideal because you can prepare it ahead. Or just serve warm crusty bread and some good-quality ham and olives. Choose a main course that is easy to prepare, cook, and serve—one-pot meals are perfect—and for dessert either ask a friend to make something or stick to a simple "assembly job."

# PORK STEAKS
## WITH APPLES
## & MUSTARD MASH

4 potatoes, peeled and diced
1 large green apple, peeled, cored, and quartered
handful of sage leaves, chopped
2 tablespoons extra virgin olive oil
1 tablespoon lemon juice
1 tablespoon honey
4 pork steaks, about 7 oz each
4 tablespoons butter
2 tablespoons milk
1 tablespoon Dijon mustard
salt and pepper

Serves **4**
Prep time **5 minutes**
Cooking time **23 minutes**

1 Cook the potatoes in a saucepan of lightly salted boiling water for 10 minutes, until tender.

2 Cut the apple quarters into thick wedges. Mix the sage with the oil, lemon juice, and honey and season to taste with salt and pepper. Mix half the flavored oil with the apple wedges and brush the remainder over the pork steaks.

3 Cook the steaks under a hot broiler for 3-4 minutes on each side, until browned and cooked through. Set aside and keep warm.

4 Drain the potatoes, mash, and beat in 3 tablespoons butter, the milk, and mustard and season to taste with salt and pepper. Keep warm.

5 Melt the remaining butter in a skillet and quickly fry the apple wedges for 2-3 minutes or until golden and softened. Serve the pork with the mustard mash, apples, and any pork juices.

# SWEET & SOUR
# PORK

**1** Mix together the egg white and pepper and coat the pork slices in the mixture. Dip each piece of pork into the cornstarch, shaking off the excess.

**2** Heat the oil in a large, nonstick skillet over a high heat until piping hot, add the pork slices, making sure there is a little space between each one, and fry for 2 minutes on each side. Turn down the heat to medium and stir-fry the pork for another 2 minutes or until done. Transfer to a serving plate and keep warm.

**3** Make the cornstarch paste. Mix the cornstarch with the water or stock to make a smooth paste without any lumps.

**4** Make the sweet and sour sauce. Combine all the ingredients in a small saucepan, bring to a boil, and thicken with the cornstarch paste. Pour the sauce over the pork and serve with rice, if desired.

1 egg white, slightly beaten
1 teaspoon black pepper
1 lb pork tenderloin or boneless
   loin, cut into ½-inch thick slices
¼ cup cornstarch
1 tablespoon canola or olive oil

**Cornstarch paste**
5 teaspoons cornstarch
¼ cup plus 1 tablespoon stock or
   water

**Sweet and sour sauce**
3 tablespoons ketchup
1 teaspoon white wine vinegar
1 cup coarsely chopped tomatoes
   (7 oz)
¼ cup pineapple juice
2 teaspoons sugar
scant 1 cup water
¾ cup pineapple pieces (5 oz)
1 large green bell pepper, cored,
   seeded, and cut into 1-inch
   pieces
1 onion, cut into 1-inch pieces
¼ cup lemon juice

Serves **2**
Prep time **20 minutes**
Cooking time **10 minutes**

**AFFORDABILITY**
**2**

### Keep your cloths clean

Admit it—you use the kitchen cloth for everything from mopping up milk to cleaning your bike chain. Damp, dirty kitchen cloths are a natural paradise for germs—a good way to zap germs is give cloths a rinse and a good squeeze, put them flat in the microwave and turn up the power for 2–3 minutes.

# BEEF *STROGANOFF*

4 tablespoons butter
3 onions, finely chopped
3 cups thinly sliced white
  mushrooms (8 oz)
1 green bell pepper, cored, seeded,
  and cut into fine strips
1 lb tenderloin steak or good
  sirloin steak, cut into strips 2
  inches long and ¼ inch thick
⅔ cup sour cream
salt and pepper
1 teaspoon chopped parsley, to
  garnish

Serves **4**
Prep time **10 minutes**
Cooking time **15 minutes**

**1** Melt half the butter in a large, deep skillet and fry the onions until pale golden. Add the mushrooms and bell pepper to the pan and cook for 5 minutes. Remove the onions, mushrooms, and bell pepper from the pan.

**2** Add the remaining butter, allow it to become hot, then fry the steak strips for about 4 minutes, turning so they are cooked evenly.

**3** Return the onions, mushrooms, and peppers to the pan and season well, then stir in the sour cream and blend well. Heat until piping hot, but do not allow to boil. Garnish with chopped parsley before serving.

AFFORDABILITY **3**

# STEAK & MUSHROOM PIE

**1** Season the flour and use it to coat the meat. Heat a dot of butter in a large, heavy skillet and fry the meat in batches until it is well browned, using a slotted spoon to drain and transfer each batch to a heatproof casserole dish. Gently fry the onion and garlic in a little more butter until softened.

**2** Add the stout, stock, bay leaves, horseradish sauce, and a little seasoning to the skillet. Bring to a boil and pour the mixture over the meat. Transfer to a preheated oven, 300°F, and cook for 1½ hours until the meat is tender.

**3** Meanwhile, fry the mushrooms in the remaining butter for 5 minutes and add them to the beef for the last 30 minutes of the cooking time. Allow to cool, then turn the meat mixture into a 4-cup pie dish and chill.

**4** Roll out the pastry until it is 2 inches larger than the dish and use it to cover the pie. Bake in a preheated oven, 375°F, for 45 minutes until deep golden.

3 tablespoons all-purpose flour
1½ lb stewing beef, diced
4 tablespoons butter
1 large onion, chopped
2 garlic cloves, crushed
scant 2 cups stout
²⁄₃ cup Beef Stock (see page 234)
2 bay leaves
1 tablespoon hot horseradish sauce
3 cups white mushrooms
9 oz shortcrust pastry (thawed if frozen)
milk, to glaze
salt and pepper

Serves **4**
Prep time **40 minutes, plus cooling**
Cooking time **2½ hours**

## Spotless microwave

It's a dirty job, but someone's got to do it. Here's an easy way: put some lemon slices in a bowl of water and microwave on high until the water is boiling (3–4 minutes). The steam will loosen the built-up grime and most of it should be easy to wipe off with a damp cloth. The bonus is your kitchen will smell nice too.

# MOUSSAKA

BRUSHING THE EGGPLANTS WITH OIL AND BROILING RATHER THAN FRYING THEM GIVES A LIGHTER, LESS "FATTY-TASTING" DISH. THE TANGY FETA TOPPING IS ALSO LOVELY AND LIGHT, BUT YOU CAN USE A MORE SUBSTANTIAL CHEESE, SUCH AS GRUYÈRE OR CHEDDAR, IF YOU PREFER.

1 lb eggplants
½ cup oil
1 large onion, finely chopped
1 lb lean ground lamb
1 14½-oz can diced tomatoes
1 teaspoon dried oregano
4 garlic cloves, crushed
⅔ cup red wine
1¼ cups Greek-style yogurt
2 eggs, beaten
3½ oz feta cheese, crumbled
salt and pepper

Serves **4**
Prep time **25 minutes**
Cooking time **1½ hours**

**1** Cut the eggplants into thin slices and arrange them in a single layer on a foil-lined broiler rack. Blend 5 tablespoons oil with plenty of salt and pepper and brush a little over the eggplants. Broil until golden, then turn and broil again, brushing with more oil. (If necessary, broil in two batches.)

**2** Heat the remaining oil in a large, heavy saucepan and fry the onion and lamb for 10 minutes until browned. Stir in the tomatoes, oregano, garlic, wine, and a little seasoning. Cover and cook gently for 20 minutes or until pulpy.

**3** Spread a quarter of the meat sauce in the base of a shallow, 2-quart heatproof dish and cover with one-third of the eggplant slices. Repeat layering, finishing with the meat sauce.

**4** Beat together the yogurt and eggs and spoon over the meat. Crumble over the feta and bake in a preheated oven, 350°F, for about 45 minutes until the topping is golden.

# STUFFED EGGPLANTS

AFFORDABILITY
2

1 Rinse and dry the eggplants. Cut them in half lengthwise and hollow out some of the flesh with a small spoon. Place the shells in a baking dish in a preheated oven, 350°F, for around 10 minutes.

2 Season the ground lamb with the cinnamon and with a little salt and pepper.

3 Heat the oil in a nonstick saucepan, add the onion, and cook until golden. Add the lamb, rice, pine nuts, mint, and chopped parsley and mix well.

4 Fill the eggplant shells with this mixture and return to the oven for around 15 minutes. If necessary, add a little water in the bottom of the dish to make sure they do not stick. Serve warm or cold.

4 eggplants
10 oz ground lamb
2 pinches of ground cinnamon
I tablespoon olive oil
1 onion, chopped
2/3 cup cooked long grain rice
2 tablespoons pine nuts
2 tablespoons finely chopped mint leaves
2 tablespoons finely chopped parsley
salt and pepper

Serves **4**
Prep time **30 minutes**
Cooking time **25 minutes**

# FISH PIE

A GOOD FISH PIE IS A CLASSIC, COMFORTING DISH THAT NEVER GOES OUT OF FASHION.

2 lb cod fillet, skinned
3 tablespoons milk
9 oz scallops or raw peeled shrimp
2½ lb potatoes, thinly sliced
2 tablespoons butter
3 large shallots, finely chopped
¼ cup chopped tarragon
¼ cup chopped parsley
4 oz Gruyère cheese, grated
Béchamel Sauce (see page 223)
salt and pepper

Serves **6**
Prep time **30 minutes**
Cooking time **1 hour**

**1** Put the cod in a skillet with the milk and seasoning. Cover and cook gently for 5 minutes. Add the scallops or shrimp and cook, covered, for an additional 2 minutes. Drain, reserving the liquid, and allow to cool.

**2** Bring a saucepan of lightly salted water to a boil, add the potatoes, return to a boil and cook for 6–8 minutes or until just tender. Drain. Melt the butter in the rinsed-out skillet and fry the shallots for 5 minutes. Stir in the herbs.

**3** Flake the fish into large chunks, discarding any bones, and arrange in a large, shallow, heatproof dish. Add the scallops or shrimp, shallots, and herbs.

**4** Stir two-thirds of the cheese into the béchamel sauce along with the poaching liquid. Pour half over the fish. Layer the potatoes over the top and pour over the remaining sauce. Sprinkle with the rest of the cheese and bake in a preheated oven, 375°F, for about 40 minutes or until golden.

AFFORDABILITY 3

# SEAFOOD
## PAELLA

2 tablespoons olive oil
1 large onion, finely diced
1 garlic clove, crushed
1 red bell pepper, cored, seeded, and chopped into ¼-inch dice
1½ cups paella rice
6¼ cups hot Fish Stock (see page 235) or water
pinch of saffron threads
2 large tomatoes, roughly chopped
10 oz raw peeled jumbo shrimp
7 oz clams, cleaned
7 oz mussels, scrubbed and beards removed
7 oz squid, cleaned and cut into rings, tentacles discarded
1 cup frozen peas, thawed
2 tablespoons chopped parsley
salt and pepper

Serves **4**
Prep time **30 minutes**
Cooking time **25 minutes**

1 Heat the oil in a large skillet, add the onion, garlic, and bell pepper and fry for a few minutes until they have started to soften. Add the rice, stir to coat, and fry for 1 minute.

2 Pour enough stock over the rice to cover it by about ½ inch. Add the saffron threads and stir well. Bring the mixture to a boil, add the tomatoes, and reduce the heat to a simmer. Stir well once again, then simmer for 10–12 minutes, stirring occasionally so that the rice does not catch on the bottom of the pan.

3 Add the shrimp, clams and mussels (discard any that do not shut when tapped), and squid to the pan, along with a little more water or stock if the rice is too dry. Cook until the clams and mussels open (discard any that do not open), the shrimp are pink, and the squid turns white and loses its transparency.

4 Stir in the peas and parsley and cook for a few more minutes until the peas are hot. Season to taste with salt and pepper and serve.

AFFORDABILITY
3

# **PAD** THAI

1 Cook the noodles in boiling water for 5 minutes until softened. Drain and immediately refresh under cold water. Drain again and set aside.

2 In a small bowl mix the soy sauce, lime juice, and fish sauce with 1 tablespoon water and set aside.

3 Heat the oil in a wok or large skillet, add the garlic and chile and stir-fry over a medium heat for 30 seconds. Add the noodles and tofu and stir-fry for 2–3 minutes or until heated through.

4 Carefully push the noodle mixture up the side of the pan, clearing the center of the pan. Add the eggs and heat gently for 1 minute without stirring, then gently start "scrambling" the eggs with a spoon. Mix the noodles back into the center and stir well until mixed with the eggs.

5 Add the soy sauce mixture and cook for 1 minute or until heated through. Stir in the bean sprouts and cilantro. Spoon into bowls, sprinkle with the peanuts, and serve immediately.

8 oz dried rice noodles
1½ tablespoons sweet soy sauce
1½ tablespoons lime juice
1 tablespoon Thai fish sauce
  (nam pla)
3 tablespoons peanut oil
2 garlic cloves, sliced
1 small red chile, seeded and
  chopped
4 oz firm tofu, diced
2 eggs, lightly beaten
1 cup bean sprouts
1 tablespoon chopped cilantro
¼ cup salted peanuts, chopped

Serves **2**
Prep time **10 minutes**
Cooking time **12 minutes**

AFFORDABILITY
2

# CHILI SHRIMP WITH
# GARLIC & SPINACH

2 tablespoons vegetable oil
1 garlic clove, sliced
1 red bird's eye chile, seeded and
  chopped
6 cups baby spinach
4 oz raw peeled jumbo shrimp
3 tablespoons light soy sauce
2 teaspoons sugar
1 tablespoon Chinese rice wine or
  dry sherry
1 tablespoon Thai fish sauce
  (nam pla)
Chinese chive flowers or chives,
  to garnish

Serves **4**
Prep time **10 minutes**
Cooking time **5 minutes**

1 Heat the oil in a wok over a high heat until the oil starts to shimmer, add the garlic and chile and stir-fry for 30 seconds.

2 Add the spinach and shrimp and stir-fry in the oil for 1–2 minutes until the spinach begins to wilt and the shrimp are pink and cooked through.

3 Mix together the soy sauce, sugar, rice wine, and fish sauce with ¼ cup plus 2 tablespoons water and add to the pan. Quickly stir-fry together for another minute, garnish with Chinese chive flowers or chives and serve while the spinach still has texture.

AFFORDABILITY
3

# SALMON
## FISHCAKES
### *WITH* SPINACH
### & POACHED EGGS

**1** Put the potatoes in a saucepan of lightly salted boiling water and cook until they can just be pierced by a sharp knife. Drain well and allow to cool.

**2** Roughly chop the salmon or process it briefly in a food processor until coarsely ground. Use a fork or the back of a wooden spoon to mash the potatoes with salt and pepper. Add the ground salmon and mix together.

**3** Flour your hands and divide the mixture into four equal pieces and press them firmly into plump fishcakes. Coat each cake in flour and chill in the refrigerator for 1 hour.

**4** Heat the oil in a large skillet, add the fishcakes, and cook for 3-4 minutes on each side.

**5** Meanwhile, put the spinach in a saucepan with just the water that clings to the leaves and cover with a lid. Heat gently for 2-3 minutes or until the spinach has just begun to wilt. Drain thoroughly and season with a little salt and pepper.

**6** Poach the eggs in a pan of gently simmering water for 3-4 minutes until just cooked. Remove the fishcakes from the pan and set them on individual plates. Top each one with some of the spinach and finish with a hot poached egg. Serve with lemon wedges.

8 oz russet potatoes, quartered
10 oz salmon fillet, skinned and
  bones removed
1-2 tablespoons all-purpose flour
½ cup sunflower or peanut oil
1 lb spinach, washed
1 tablespoon vinegar
4 eggs
sea salt and pepper
lemon wedges, to serve

Serves **4**
Prep time **20 minutes, plus chilling**
Cooking time **25 minutes**

# BROILED HADDOCK
## WITH LENTILS & SPINACH

2 teaspoons olive oil
1 onion, finely chopped
pinch of ground cumin
pinch of ground turmeric
pinch of dried red pepper flakes
1 8-oz can lentils, rinsed and
    drained
3¾ cups baby spinach leaves
4 tablespoons sour cream
2 skinless haddock fillets, about
    4 oz each
lemon wedges, to garnish
broiled tomatoes, to serve

Serves **2**
Prep time **10 minutes**
Cooking time **15 minutes**

1 Heat half the oil in a nonstick skillet, add the onions, and cook for about 5 minutes until softened. Add the cumin, turmeric, and pepper flakes and cook, stirring, for 1 minute. Add the lentils, spinach, and sour cream and cook gently for 4–5 minutes until the spinach has wilted.

2 Meanwhile, brush both sides of the haddock with the remaining oil, put on a nonstick baking sheet, and cook under a preheated high broiler for 2–3 minutes on each side until just cooked through.

3 Arrange the lentil and spinach mixture on warm serving plates and top with the haddock. Garnish with lemon wedges and serve with broiled tomatoes.

# CREAMY FISH
## *Lasagna*

CHUNKY, SUCCULENT PIECES OF FISH ARE A MUST FOR THIS DISH SO THEY'RE NOT COMPLETELY LOST BETWEEN THE LAYERS OF PASTA AND SAUCE. IF YOU USE DRIED LASAGNA SHEETS COOK THEM FIRST UNTIL THEY ARE JUST TENDER.

**1** Put the tomatoes, onion, garlic, tomato paste, and a little seasoning in a large saucepan and bring to a boil. Cook for about 10 minutes or until the mixture is thick and pulpy. Stir in half the anchovies and lay the haddock on top. Cook gently for 5 minutes or until the fish is opaque.

**2** Spoon one-third of the mixture into a shallow, 5-cup heatproof dish, making sure the pieces of fish are evenly distributed. Arrange a layer of lasagna sheets on top. Cover with half the remaining tomato and fish mixture and spoon over one-third of the cheese sauce. Place another layer of lasagna sheets on top and cover with the remaining tomatoes and fish. Add the remaining lasagna sheets and spoon over the rest of the sauce.

**3** Tear the bread into pieces and blend in a food processor to make coarse bread crumbs. Add the remaining anchovies and blend again until mixed.

**4** Sprinkle the bread crumbs over the lasagna and drizzle with the oil. Bake in a preheated oven, 350°F, for about 45 minutes or until golden. Allow to stand for 10 minutes before serving.

2 14½-oz each cans diced tomatoes
1 large onion, finely chopped
2 garlic cloves, crushed
3 tablespoons sun-dried tomato paste
1 2-oz can anchovy fillets in olive oil, drained and chopped
1½ lb skinned haddock fillet, cut into chunks
4 oz fresh lasagna sheets
Rich Cheese Sauce (see page 224)
2 slices of bread
2 tablespoons olive oil
salt and pepper

Serves **4-5**
Prep time **25 minutes, plus standing**
Cooking time **1 hour**

# CHERRY TOMATO & RICOTTA PENNE

10 oz dried penne
3 tablespoons olive oil
1 onion, chopped
4 garlic cloves, crushed
1 tablespoon chopped oregano
1½ cups cherry tomatoes, halved
1 teaspoon sugar
3 tablespoons sun-dried tomato
    paste
1 cup ricotta cheese
salt and pepper

Serves **4**
Prep time **5 minutes**
Cooking time **10 minutes**

1 Cook the pasta in a large saucepan of lightly salted boiling water for about 10 minutes or until just tender.

2 Meanwhile, heat the oil in a skillet, add the onion, and fry gently for 3 minutes. Add the garlic, oregano, tomatoes, and sugar and fry quickly, stirring, for 1 minute. Add the tomato paste and 6 tablespoons of water, season to taste with salt and pepper, and bring to a boil. Add dessertspoonfuls of the ricotta cheese to the pan and heat through gently for 1 minute.

3 Drain the pasta and pile onto serving plates. Spoon the tomato and cheese mixture on top, taking care not to break up the ricotta too much. Serve immediately.

AFFORDABILITY 1

### Buy in bulk

Look out for bulk-buy specials on dry goods such as pasta, rice, cereal, jars, and cans. They will usually last for a few months, and you could save yourself a fortune on food that you know you're going to use—as long as you've got room under your bed for ten trays of baked beans.

# RIBBON PASTA WITH EGGPLANTS
## & PINE NUTS

1 Heat the oil in a large skillet or sauté pan and fry the eggplants and onions for 8–10 minutes until golden and tender. Add the pine nuts and garlic and fry for 2 minutes. Stir in the tomato paste and stock and cook for 2 minutes.

2 Meanwhile, cook the pasta in a large saucepan of lightly salted boiling water for 2 minutes or until just tender.

3 Drain the pasta and return to the pan. Add the sauce and olives, season to taste with salt and pepper, and toss together over a moderate heat for 1 minute until combined. Sprinkle with the parsley and serve immediately.

½ cup olive oil
2 eggplants, diced
2 red onions, sliced
½ cup pine nuts
3 garlic cloves, crushed
¼ cup plus 1 tablespoon sun-dried tomato paste
⅔ cup Vegetable Stock (see page 235)
10 oz fresh ribbon pasta
½ cup pitted black olives
salt and pepper
3 tablespoons coarsely chopped flat leaf parsley, to garnish

Serves **4**
Prep time **5 minutes**
Cooking time **17-20 minutes**

AFFORDABILITY

AFFORDABILITY 1

# CHERRY TOMATO **TARTS** WITH **PESTO CREAM**

2 tablespoons extra virgin olive oil
1 onion, finely chopped
1½ cups cherry tomatoes
2 garlic cloves, crushed
3 tablespoons sun-dried tomato paste
11 oz prepared puff pastry (thawed if frozen)
beaten egg, to glaze
⅔ cup sour cream
2 tablespoons Pesto (see page 228)
salt and pepper
basil leaves, to garnish

Serves **4**
Prep time **10 minutes**
Cooking time **18 minutes**

1 Lightly grease a large baking sheet and sprinkle with water. Heat the oil in a skillet, add the onion, and fry for about 3 minutes until softened. Halve about ten of the tomatoes. Remove the pan from the heat, add the garlic and tomato paste, then stir in all the tomatoes, turning until they are lightly coated in the sauce.

2 Place the pastry on a lightly floured surface and cut out four 5-inch rounds, using a cutter or small bowl as a guide. Transfer to the baking sheet and use the tip of a sharp knife to make a shallow cut ½ inch from the edge of each round to form a rim. (Do not cut all the way through the pastry.) Brush the rims with beaten egg. Pile the tomato mixture on the centers of the pastry circles making sure the mixture stays within the rims. Bake the tarts in a preheated oven, 425°F, for about 15 minutes until the pastry is risen and golden.

3 Meanwhile, lightly mix together the sour cream, pesto, and salt and pepper in a bowl so that the sour cream is streaked with the pesto.

4 Transfer the cooked tarts to serving plates and spoon over the sour cream and pesto mixture. Serve sprinkled with basil leaves.

# MUSHROOM & BROCCOLI PIE

1 Cook the broccoli in a large saucepan of lightly salted boiling water for about 2 minutes or until the florets are just beginning to soften.

2 Meanwhile, heat the oil in a large skillet and cook the mushrooms over a medium heat, stirring occasionally, for about 5 minutes. Stir in the Gorgonzola, mascarpone, and sour cream. Add the drained broccoli florets and the chives and season to taste with salt and pepper. Spoon the mixture into four individual heatproof dishes or a single large rectangular heatproof dish.

3 Lay the pastry over the filling, pressing it to the sides of the dish to seal. Brush the top with beaten egg and cut two slits in the pastry to allow steam to escape. Cook in a preheated oven, 425°F, for about 25 minutes until the pastry is crisp and golden. Serve immediately.

1½ cups broccoli florets
3 tablespoons olive oil
4½ cups trimmed and thickly
   sliced mushrooms (11½ oz)
5 oz Gorgonzola cheese
3 tablespoons mascarpone cheese
¼ cup sour cream
2 tablespoons chopped chives
1 large sheet prepared puff pastry
   (thawed if frozen)
1 egg, lightly beaten
salt and pepper

Serves **4**
Prep time **8 minutes**
Cooking time **30 minutes**

# VEGETABLE BOLOGNESE

½ tablespoon vegetable oil
1 onion, chopped
1 7-oz can baby carrots, drained and chopped
1 leek, sliced
2 celery sticks, sliced
1 14½-oz can diced tomatoes
1 tablespoon tomato paste
1 teaspoon cayenne pepper
1½ cups sliced mushrooms (4 oz)
12 oz spaghetti
salt and pepper
basil leaves, to garnish

Serves **4**
Prep time **10 minutes**
Cooking time **15 minutes**

1 Heat the oil in a saucepan, add the onion, and fry over a low heat for 3–5 minutes or until soft. Stir in the carrots, leek, and celery. Add the tomatoes, tomato paste, cayenne pepper, and mushrooms and stir to combine. Season to taste with salt and pepper and simmer for 10 minutes.

2 Meanwhile, cook the spaghetti in a large saucepan of lightly salted boiling water for 8–10 minutes or according to the package directions until just tender. Drain the pasta and sprinkle with pepper.

3 Mound the spaghetti on serving plates, spoon the sauce over the top, and serve garnished with a few basil leaves.

AFFORDABILITY **1**

## Pep up pasta sauces

Spruce up cheap jars of pasta sauce with a handful of olives, a sprinkle of dried red pepper flakes, or a few chopped herbs. Cans of diced tomatoes also tend to be fairly cheap, so you can add the same to these and enjoy a budget meal with a bit of pizzazz for just a few more cents.

# SPINACH, ONION & CREAM CHEESE PIZZA

**1** Lightly grease a large baking sheet. Put the flour in a bowl with the oil and salt. Add a scant ½ cup water and mix to a soft dough, adding a little more water, a teaspoonful at a time, if the dough is too dry. Roll out on a floured surface into a circle about 11 inches across. Put the dough circle on the baking sheet and bake in a preheated oven, 450°F, for 5 minutes until a crust has formed.

**2** Make the topping. Beat together the cream cheese, sour cream, rosemary, and a little salt and pepper.

**3** Heat the oil in a skillet and fry the onion for 3-4 minutes or until softened. Add the spinach and a little salt and pepper and cook, stirring, for about 1 minute until the spinach has just wilted.

**4** Pile the spinach onto the pizza base, spreading it to within ½ inch of the edge. Place spoonfuls of the cheese mixture over the spinach. Bake for an additional 8 minutes or until turning golden.

3 tablespoons olive oil, plus extra
   for greasing
2 cups self-rising flour
1 teaspoon salt

**Topping**
scant ½ cup full-fat cream cheese
scant ½ cup sour cream
2 teaspoons chopped rosemary
3 tablespoons olive oil
1 large onion, finely sliced
7 cups young spinach
salt and pepper

Serves **4**
Prep time **25 minutes**
Cooking time **15 minutes**

# **PIZZA** FIORENTINA

1 tablespoon olive oil, plus extra
  for drizzling and glazing
2 garlic cloves, crushed
1 lb baby spinach
all-purpose flour, for dusting
4 store-bought pizza bases,
  about 9 inches across
scant 1 cup diced tomatoes,
  seived
7 oz mozzarella cheese, drained
  and chopped
20 black olives
4 eggs
salt and pepper

Serves **4**
Prep time **20 minutes**
Cooking time **40 minutes**

**1** Heat the oil in a large skillet with the garlic for 15 seconds. Add the spinach and cook over a high heat for 1–2 minutes until just wilted. Season lightly with salt and pepper.

**2** Put a baking sheet in a preheated oven, 475°F. Put a pizza base in a well-floured, 9-inch loose-bottomed tart pan.

**3** Spoon 3 tablespoons diced tomatoes over the base and sprinkle with a quarter of the mozzarella, spinach, and olives. Crack 1 egg onto the pizza, drizzle with oil, and season lightly with salt and pepper. Brush the border with oil to glaze, if desired. Remove the baking sheet from the oven, slide the pan onto it and quickly return to the oven. Bake for 7–8 minutes until cooked and bubbling. Serve immediately. As the first pizza cooks, prepare the next for the oven.

AFFORDABILITY
1

# PIZZA PUFF PIES

AFFORDABILITY
1

1 Heat the oil in saucepan, add the onion, and fry for 5 minutes until softened. Add the garlic, tomatoes, and sugar and season to taste with salt and pepper. Cover and simmer gently for 15 minutes, stirring from time to time until the sauce has thickened. Allow to cool slightly.

2 Cut the pastry into six pieces. Roll out each piece on a lightly floured surface and trim to a 6-inch circle using a saucer or cutter as a guide. Press each pastry circle into the base of a lightly oiled metal tart pan, 4 inches across and 1 inch deep, and press the pastry at intervals to the sides of the pan to give a wavy edge.

3 Keeping about half the smaller basil leaves for garnish, tear the larger leaves into pieces and stir into the sauce. Divide the sauce between the pies and spread to give an even layer. Cut the mozzarella into six slices and add a slice to each pizza. Sprinkle the mozzarella with a little salt and pepper and add an olive to each, if desired.

4 Bake in a preheated oven, 400°F, for 20 minutes until the pastry is crisp and golden. Allow to cool for 5 minutes, then turn out. Drizzle with a little olive oil, if desired, and sprinkle with the remaining basil leaves. Serve warm with salad.

1 tablespoon olive oil
1 onion, chopped
1 garlic clove, finely chopped
1 14½-oz can diced tomatoes
1 teaspoon sugar
1 lb puff pastry (thawed if frozen)
small bunch of basil
4 oz mozzarella cheese, drained
6 pitted black olives (optional)
salt and pepper

**To serve**
olive oil (optional)
green salad

Makes **6**
Prep time **25 minutes**
Cooking time **40 minutes**

# GRILLED ZUCCHINI
## *with* GOAT CHEESE

5 large zucchini, diagonally sliced
2 tablespoons extra virgin olive oil
1-2 garlic cloves, finely diced
3½ oz soft goat cheese
¼ cup pine nuts, toasted
salt and pepper

Serves **4**
Prep time **10 minutes**
Cooking time **5 minutes**

1 Brush the zucchini slices with 1 tablespoon oil and cook in a hot ridged grill pan for 1-2 minutes each side. The zucchini should be cooked but still firm. Season to taste with salt and pepper.

2 Heat the remaining oil in a small skillet over a medium heat and gently fry the garlic for 1 minute.

3 Transfer the zucchini to a warm serving plate and crumble over the goat cheese. Sprinkle with the pine nuts and drizzle the garlic oil on top. Serve immediately.

AFFORDABILITY
2

# PESTO
# ALLA
# GENOVESE

IN GENOA, THE HOME OF PESTO, THIS AROMATIC PASTA IS TRADITIONALLY COOKED WITH POTATOES AND GREEN BEANS. THIS MIGHT SOUND UNUSUAL, BUT IT IS TRULY A HEAVENLY COMBINATION.

1 cup basil leaves
3 tablespoons pine nuts
2 garlic cloves, crushed
2 tablespoons grated Parmesan
cheese, plus extra to serve
1 tablespoon grated pecorino
cheese
3 tablespoons olive oil
8 oz potatoes, peeled and thinly
sliced
13 oz dried trenette or linguine
1¼ cups green beans

Serves **4**
Prep time **30 minutes**
Cooking time **20 minutes**

1 Use a mortar and pestle to grind together the basil, pine nuts, and garlic to form a paste. Stir in the cheeses, then slowly add the oil, a little at a time, stirring all the time with a wooden spoon. Alternatively, blend the basil, pine nuts, and garlic in a food processor until the mixture forms a paste. Add the cheeses and process briefly. Then, with the motor still running, pour in the oil through the feed tube in a thin, steady stream.

2 Cook the potatoes in a large saucepan of lightly salted boiling water for 5 minutes, then add the pasta and cook according to the package directions or until just tender. Add the beans 5 minutes before the end of the cooking time.

3 Drain the pasta and vegetables, reserving 2 tablespoons of the cooking water. Return the cooked pasta and vegetables to the pan and stir in the pesto sauce, adding as much of the reserved water as needed to loosen the mixture. Serve immediately, sprinkled with some extra grated Parmesan.

# ROAST POTATOES WITH ROSEMARY & GARLIC

AFFORDABILITY
1

1 Cut the potatoes lengthwise into quarters and pat them dry on paper towels.

2 Put half the oil in a large roasting pan and place in a preheated oven, 450°F.

3 Mix together the remaining oil and the rosemary and toss the potatoes in the oil to coat them completely. Add the potatoes to the roasting pan in the oven, shake carefully so they are in an even layer, then place the pan at the top of the oven and cook for 20 minutes.

4 Remove the pan from the oven and turn the potatoes so that they cook evenly. Sprinkle the garlic among the potatoes, return the pan to the oven and cook for another 5 minutes. Remove the potatoes from the oven, season with salt and pepper, and serve immediately.

1½ lb potatoes, unpeeled
¼ cup olive oil
2 tablespoons chopped rosemary
4 garlic cloves, thinly sliced
salt and pepper

Serves **4**
Prep time **5 minutes**
Cooking time **25 minutes**

# PATATAS
## *Bravas*

THIS VERSION OF THE CLASSIC SPANISH DISH USES A THICK, RICH TOMATO SAUCE, WHILE THE POTATOES RETAIN THEIR CRISP, APPETIZING TEXTURE.

¼ cup plus 1 tablespoon olive oil
1 lb 10 oz potatoes, cubed
1 red onion, chopped
2 bay leaves
½ teaspoon hot paprika
2 garlic cloves, crushed
4 tomatoes, skinned and chopped
2 tablespoons sun-dried tomato paste
salt
3 tablespoons flat leaf parsley, coarsely chopped, to garnish

Serves **6**
Prep time **20 minutes**
Cooking time **25 minutes**

**1** Heat 3 tablespoons oil in a large skillet, add the potatoes and a pinch of salt and fry gently, stirring frequently, for 15 minutes until golden.

**2** Meanwhile, in a separate pan heat the remaining oil and fry the onion with the bay leaves for 5 minutes. Add the paprika and garlic and fry for another minute.

**3** Stir in the tomatoes, tomato paste, half the parsley, and 2 tablespoons water. Cover and cook for 8-10 minutes, stirring occasionally to break up the tomatoes.

**4** Add the tomato sauce to the potatoes and cook for an additional 5 minutes, adding a dash of water if the sauce loses its juiciness. Check the seasoning, garnish with parsley, and serve hot.

AFFORDABILITY
**1**

# GRILLED VEGETABLE *&* HALOUMI SALAD

**1** Put the tomatoes and mushrooms in a roasting pan, drizzle with about 2 tablespoons oil, season to taste with salt and pepper, and cook in a preheated oven, 350°F, for 10 minutes.

**2** Meanwhile, cut the zucchini into batons about 1½ x ¾ inches and put them in a large bowl with the trimmed asparagus. Drizzle with olive oil and a pinch of salt and pepper.

**3** Heat a ridged grill pan over a high heat and grill the asparagus and zucchini. Transfer the asparagus and zucchini to the oven with the other vegetables and cook for an additional 6–8 minutes.

**4** Cut the haloumi into ¼-inch slices. Heat 1 teaspoon olive oil in a large skillet over a medium heat and cook the cheese slices until golden.

**5** Make the dressing by beating the oil and vinegar. Stack the vegetables on serving plates, top with slices of cheese, spoon over the dressing, and serve.

12 cherry tomatoes on the vine
4 portobello mushrooms
2–3 tablespoons olive oil
2 zucchini
1 lb asparagus
8 oz haloumi cheese
salt and pepper

**Dressing**
2 tablespoons olive oil
2 tablespoons balsamic vinegar

Serves **4**
Prep time **15 minutes**
Cooking time **25 minutes**

AFFORDABILITY
1

# MINT & LEMON GRASS TEA

THIS CALMING TEA STIMULATES THE DIGESTION, SO IT'S PERFECT FOR SERVING TO GUESTS AFTER A LARGE MEAL.

4 lemon grass stalks, lightly
crushed to release the oils
small handful of mint leaves
1 tablespoon honey (optional)

Serves **4**
Prep time **5 minutes, plus
infusing**
Cooking time **5-6 minutes**

1 Bring 3 cups water to a boil in a large saucepan. Add the lemon grass stalks and boil for 5-6 minutes. Remove from the heat.

2 Add the mint leaves and honey, if desired, cover, and allow to infuse for 10 minutes.

3 Serve in cups or glasses. If you prefer, serve the mixture chilled, in a tall glass with plenty of ice.

# GREEN TEA

1 Put ¾-1 teaspoon green tea leaves (to taste, whether strong or weak) in a cup. Boil the water, but wait 3 minutes before pouring it over the leaves.

2 Add the water and allow to infuse for 1-5 minutes. To add more fragrance, put a few fresh mint leaves or any other herb or spice (such as saffron, mint, orange tree blossoms, or cloves) into the cup. The tea is best drunk without sugar.

¾-1 teaspoon green tea leaves
small handful of fresh herbs or
   spices (optional)

Serves **1**
Prep time **2 minutes, plus
infusing**

AFFORDABILITY

1

CORN & PEPPER FRITTATA

CHICKEN WITH SWEET
POTATO WEDGES

EGG-FRIED RICE

CAULIFLOWER CHEESE

# STRAPPED FOR CASH

# SOUTHERN FRIED CHICKEN

1 lb sweet potatoes, peeled
1 lb baking potatoes, scrubbed
¼ cup plus 2 tablespoons
  sunflower oil
1½ teaspoons smoked paprika
1½ teaspoons dried oregano
1 teaspoon powdered mustard
1 teaspoon dried red pepper flakes
¼ cup all-purpose flour
2 eggs, beaten
2½ cups fresh bread crumbs
4 chicken thigh and drumstick
  joints
salt and pepper

**To serve**
mayonnaise
green salad

Serves **4**
Prep time **25 minutes**
Cooking time **35-40 minutes**

1 Thickly slice the sweet and baking potatoes and cut them into thick wedges. Mix 3 tablespoons oil with 1 teaspoon paprika, 1 teaspoon oregano, ½ teaspoon mustard, ½ teaspoon red pepper flakes and some salt in a large plastic bag or bowl. Add the potatoes and toss in the mixture to coat.

2 Mix the remaining paprika, oregano, mustard, and red pepper flakes with the flour on a large plate and season to taste. Mix the eggs with 2 tablespoons water in a shallow dish and put the bread crumbs on a second large plate.

3 Coat the chicken pieces in the flour mixture, then the beaten egg, and then the bread crumbs until completely covered.

4 Heat a large roasting pan in a preheated oven, 400°F, for 5 minutes. Meanwhile, heat the remaining oil in a large skillet, add the chicken, and fry until pale golden. Transfer the chicken to the hot roasting pan, add the potatoes, and roast for 30-35 minutes until the chicken is cooked through and the potatoes, are crisp and golden. Transfer to serving plates and serve with mayonnaise and salad.

# CHICKEN WITH
## PEANUT SAUCE

1 Heat a ridged grill pan or ordinary nonstick skillet, add the chicken breasts, and cook for 8-10 minutes on each side.

2 Meanwhile, put the soy sauce, peanut butter, lemon juice, and a little pepper in a small saucepan. Mix with 4 tablespoons water and heat gently, adjusting the consistency of the sauce with a little more water if necessary so that it is slightly runny but coats the back of a spoon.

3 When the chicken is cooked, serve with the peanut sauce drizzled over the top, garnished with cilantro and chopped fried peanuts, if desired. Serve with mixed vegetable noodles.

4 boneless, skinless chicken breasts, about 4 oz each
1 tablespoon soy sauce
2 tablespoons crunchy or smooth peanut butter
¼ cup lemon juice
pepper

**To garnish**
cilantro leaves
peanuts, fried, chopped (optional)

Serves **4**
Prep time **5 minutes**
Cooking time **16-20 minutes**

AFFORDABILITY

2

# *FAST* CHICKEN **CURRY**

3 tablespoons olive oil
1 onion, finely chopped
¼ cup medium curry paste
8 boneless, skinless chicken
   thighs, cut into thin strips
1 14½-oz can diced tomatoes
8 oz broccoli, broken into small
   florets, and stalks peeled and
   sliced
scant ½ cup coconut milk
salt and pepper

**1** Heat the oil in a deep, nonstick saucepan, add the onion, and cook for 3 minutes until soft. Add the curry paste and cook, stirring, for 1 minute.

**2** Add the chicken, tomatoes, broccoli, and coconut milk to the pan. Bring to a boil, reduce the heat, cover, and cook over a low heat for 15-20 minutes.

**3** Remove from the heat, season well with salt and pepper, and serve immediately.

Serves **4**
Prep time **5 minutes**
Cooking time **20-25 minutes**

AFFORDABILITY 1

# JERK
## CHICKEN WINGS

**1** Put the chicken wings in a nonmetallic dish. In a small bowl beat together the oil, jerk seasoning mix, lemon juice, and salt. Pour the mixture over the chicken and stir well until evenly coated. Cover and allow to marinate in the refrigerator for at least 30 minutes or overnight.

**2** Arrange the chicken wings on a broiler rack and cook under a preheated broiler, basting halfway through cooking with any remaining marinade, for 6 minutes on each side or until cooked through, tender, and lightly charred at the edges. Increase or reduce the temperature setting of the broiler if necessary to make sure that the wings cook through. Garnish with chopped parsley and serve immediately with lemon wedges for squeezing over.

12 large chicken wings
2 tablespoons olive oil
1 tablespoon jerk seasoning mix
2 tablespoons lemon juice
1 teaspoon salt
chopped flat leaf parsley, to
　garnish
lemon wedges, to serve

Serves **4**
Prep time **5 minutes, plus marinating**
Cooking time **12 minutes**

# CHICKEN WITH
## SWEET POTATO
# WEDGES

4 sweet potatoes, about 2½ lb in
   total, scrubbed
4 boneless, skinless chicken
   thighs, cut into chunks
1 red onion, cut into wedges
4 plum tomatoes, cut into chunks
5 oz chorizo in one piece, skinned,
   sliced or diced depending on
   diameter
3 rosemary sprigs, leaves torn
   from stems
¼ cup olive oil
salt and pepper
watercress salad, to serve
   (optional)

Serves **4**
Prep time **20 minutes**
Cooking time **35 minutes**

1 Cut the potatoes in half and then into thick wedges. Put them into a large roasting pan with the chicken, onion, and tomatoes. Tuck the chorizo in and around the potatoes, then sprinkle with the rosemary and some salt and pepper.

2 Drizzle over the oil and cook in a preheated oven, 400°F, for about 35 minutes, turning once or twice until the chicken is golden and cooked through and the potato wedges are browned and tender.

3 Spoon onto serving plates and serve as it is, or with a watercress salad.

# STEAK MEATLOAF

SERVE THIS MEATLOAF HOT OR COLD, DEPENDING ON THE WEATHER AND CIRCUMSTANCES. LEFTOVERS, ACCOMPANIED WITH SALAD AND CHUTNEY, MAKE AN IDEAL LUNCHTIME SNACK.

**1** Put the peppers and onion in a roasting pan, shake gently so they are in an even layer, drizzle with the oil, and cook in a preheated oven, 400°F, for 30 minutes until lightly roasted. Chop roughly when they are cooked. Reduce the heat to 325°F.

**2** Use some bacon to line the base and long sides of a 2-quart loaf pan, overlapping them slightly and letting the ends overhang the sides. Finely chop the rest.

**3** Mix together the ground steak and pork, chopped bacon, roasted vegetables, herbs, Worcestershire sauce, tomato paste, bread crumbs, egg, and seasoning. Pack the mixture into the pan and fold the ends of the bacon over the filling. Cover with kitchen foil, place in a roasting pan and pour in boiling water to a depth of ¾ inch. Cook in the oven for 2 hours.

**4** To serve hot leave for 15 minutes, then invert onto a serving plate. To serve cold allow to cool in the pan, then remove and wrap in foil.

2 red bell peppers, cored, seeded, and cut into chunks
1 red onion, sliced
3 tablespoons olive oil
10 oz thin-cut bacon
1 lb lean ground steak
8 oz ground pork
2 tablespoons chopped oregano
2 tablespoons chopped parsley
3 tablespoons Worcestershire sauce
2 tablespoons sun-dried tomato paste
1 cup fresh bread crumbs
1 egg
salt and pepper

Serves **6**
Prep time **30 minutes**
Cooking time **2½ hours**

AFFORDABILITY
2

2 tablespoons oil
1 lb lean ground lamb
1 onion, finely chopped
2 carrots, finely chopped
2 celery sticks, finely chopped
1 garlic clove, finely chopped
1 tablespoon all-purpose flour
1¼ cups Chicken or Lamb Stock
  (see page 234)
2 tablespoons tomato paste
1 16-oz can baked beans
2 lb potatoes
4 tablespoons butter
3-4 tablespoons milk
¼ cup grated cheddar cheese
  (optional)
salt and pepper

Serves **4**
Prep time **20 minutes**
Cooking time **1 hour 20
minutes-1½ hours**

AFFORDABILITY
**1**

# SHEPHERD'S PIE

**1** Heat the oil in a large, heavy saucepan and fry the lamb, stirring, until lightly browned. Add the vegetables and garlic and fry for 5 minutes.

**2** Stir in the flour, stock, and tomato paste, season to taste with salt and pepper and heat until bubbling. Cook gently for 30 minutes until the lamb is tender, adding a little water or more stock if the mixture starts to dry out. Stir in the beans and turn into a shallow heatproof dish.

**3** Meanwhile, cook the potatoes in a large saucepan of lightly salted boiling water until tender. Drain and return to the pan. Mash well with the butter, milk, and seasoning. Spoon the mashed potato over the meat mixture, spreading it in an even layer with a fork. Cook in a preheated oven, 375°F, for 30-40 minutes until pale golden.

**4** For a crispy crust pop the pie under the broiler before serving, with or without a sprinkling of grated cheese.

# SAUSAGE
# MEATBALLS,
## PEAS & PASTA

1 Cut the sausages into small pieces and roll into walnut-size balls.

2 Heat half the oil in a large, nonstick skillet, add the meatballs, and cook over a medium heat, stirring frequently, for 10 minutes until cooked through. Remove from the pan with a slotted spoon.

3 Meanwhile, plunge the pasta into a large saucepan of lightly salted boiling water. Return to a boil and cook for 8 minutes. Add the peas, return to a boil and cook for another 2 minutes until the peas and pasta are just tender. Drain well, reserving 1/4 cup of the cooking water.

4 Add the garlic, sage, and pepper flakes to the meatball pan, season to taste with salt and pepper, and cook over a low heat for 2–3 minutes until the garlic is soft but not browned. Return the meatballs to the pan and stir.

5 Return the pasta and peas to the saucepan and stir in the meatball mixture, reserved cooking water, and remaining oil and heat through for 2 minutes. Serve in bowls topped with grated Parmesan.

1 lb beef or pork sausages, skins removed
1/4 cup extra virgin olive oil
13 oz dried fusilli
1 2/3 cups frozen peas (thawed)
2 garlic cloves, sliced
2 tablespoons chopped sage
1/2 teaspoon red pepper flakes
salt and black pepper
grated Parmesan cheese, to serve

Serves **4**
Prep time **20 minutes**
Cooking time **15 minutes**

# BEEF GOULASH

¼ cup olive oil
3 lb braising beef, cubed
2 onions, sliced
2 red bell peppers, cored, seeded
    and diced
1 tablespoon smoked paprika
2 tablespoons chopped marjoram
1 teaspoon caraway seeds
4 cups Beef Stock (see page 234)
¼ cup plus 1 tablespoon tomato
    paste
salt and pepper

Serves **8**
Prep time **10 minutes**
Cooking time **2-2½ hours**

1 Heat the oil in a large, heavy saucepan, add the beef, in three batches, and cook over a high heat for 5 minutes until browned all over. Remove from the pan with a slotted spoon.

2 Add the onions and bell peppers to the pan and cook gently for 10 minutes until softened. Stir in the paprika, marjoram, and caraway seeds and cook, stirring, for another minute.

3 Return the beef to the pan, add the stock, tomato paste, and salt and pepper to taste and bring to a boil, stirring. Reduce the heat, cover, and simmer gently for 1½-2 hours. Remove the lid for the final 30 minutes if the sauce needs thickening.

## Double up and freeze

If you're cooking a spaghetti Bolognese, chili, or curry, double up on the ingredients and freeze half. It won't take any longer to cook but you'll have a ready-prepared meal in the freezer for the next time you can't be bothered to cook, or can't afford a trip to the shops.

# MONEY
## MATTERS

◇◇◇◇◇◇◇◇◇◇◇◇◇◇◇◇◇◇◇◇◇◇◇◇◇◇◇◇◇◇◇◇◇◇◇◇◇◇◇◇◇◇◇◇◇◇◇◇◇◇◇◇◇◇◇◇◇◇◇◇◇

Budget. It's a nasty word, but it's one you'll be hearing a lot during your time at college. With fees and loan repayments threatening to soak up your disposable income as soon as you land a job, you need to do everything you can to make your meager funds stretch as far as possible.

## BILLS, BILLS, BILLS

This can often be a bone of contention in student households, with loose change being counted out every time a utility bill arrives. You can save yourselves a lot of hassle (and some money) by switching all your utility bills to direct debit so that you know exactly how much you're paying each month, and you won't get any nasty surprises after a bitterly cold winter in a energy-inefficient house. If there are just two or three of you it's worth getting a household bank account, with each of you paying in a monthly sum to cover all the household expenses.

If you're shopping independently make food ownership rights clear from the start—a piece of cake or coveted pint of milk could cause a major incident if one person doesn't respect the food rules. However, if you plan to shop as a household then it's a good idea to have someone who doesn't mind taking charge of collecting money and making a communal shopping list. The total food budget will obviously depend on where you live and what supermarkets, markets, and so on are nearby.

Clubbing together can work out a lot cheaper because you can buy bigger (so more economical) packages of cereal, margarine, cartons of milk, and vegetables. Here are a few more tips to make your food budget stretch even further:

- Wait for closing time at the supermarket—that's when the prices drop.

- Look out for BOGOF deals (that's buy one, get one free, to you and me).

- Ditch take-outs in favor of supermarket equivalents, much cheaper.

- Make your own lunch—okay, it's not as cool as a latte and ciabatta at the canteen, but you'll save a fortune.

If there's a sell-by date food bargain, buy it and freeze it for another time.

Choose all the food you want online so you know exactly how much it will cost. Then go and buy it yourself and save on the delivery charge.

# CALF'S LIVER & BACON

FRY THE LIVER A LITTLE LONGER THAN SUGGESTED IN THE RECIPE IF YOU PREFER IT COOKED THROUGH, BUT TAKE CARE NOT TO COOK IT FOR TOO LONG OR IT WILL START TO TOUGHEN UP.

2 teaspoons all-purpose flour
1½ lb calf's liver
2 tablespoons butter
1 tablespoon olive oil
12 large sage leaves
8 Canadian bacon slices
⅔ cup hard cider
salt and pepper

Serves **4**
Prep time **10 minutes**
Cooking time **6-8 minutes**

1 Season the flour with salt and pepper. Cut away any tubes from the liver and dust it with the flour.

2 Melt half the butter with the oil in a large skillet until bubbling. Add the sage leaves and cook for about 30 seconds until sizzling. Drain and transfer to a plate with a slotted spoon.

3 Fry the bacon until golden, drain and transfer to the plate and keep warm. Add the liver to the pan and fry for about 2 minutes until deep golden. Turn the slices and return the bacon and sage to the pan. Cook for an additional 1-2 minutes. (At this stage the liver will be slightly pink in the center but cook a little more if preferred.) Drain and keep warm.

4 Add the cider to the pan and let it bubble until slightly reduced, scraping up any residue. Beat in the remaining butter and check the seasoning. Transfer the liver and bacon to serving plates, spoon over the sauce, and sprinkle with the sage leaves.

# EGG-FRIED
# RICE

1 Put the eggs, ginger, and half the soy sauce in a bowl and beat lightly to combine.

2 Heat the oil in a wok over a high heat until the oil starts to shimmer. Pour in the egg mixture and use a spatula to scramble it for 30-60 seconds, until just cooked.

3 Add the cold cooked rice, green onions, sesame oil, and remaining soy sauce and stir-fry for 1-2 minutes or until the rice is steaming hot.

4 eggs
2 teaspoons chopped fresh ginger root
1½ tablespoons light soy sauce
2 tablespoons peanut oil
2¼ cups cold cooked jasmine rice
2 green onions, finely sliced
¼ teaspoon sesame oil

Serves **2**
Prep time **5 minutes**
Cooking time **4 minutes**

AFFORDABILITY

# CROQUE MONSIEUR

7 tablespoons butter, softened
8 slices of white bread
4 slices of cheddar cheese
4 slices of cooked ham
4 tablespoons vegetable oil
pepper

Serves **4**
Prep time **10 minutes**
Cooking time **10 minutes**

1 Spread half the butter over one side of each slice of bread. Put a slice of cheddar on four of the buttered slices, top with a slice of ham, and sprinkle with pepper. Top with the remaining slices of bread, butter side down, and press down hard.

2 Melt half the rest of the butter with half the oil in a large skillet, and fry two sandwiches until golden brown, turning once. Cook the remaining sandwiches in the same way, cut into halves, and serve immediately.

AFFORDABILITY
1

# BLT
## *Sandwich*

1 Heat a small, nonstick skillet and cook the bacon, turning once, until it is golden brown and crisp. Remove and drain on paper towels.

2 Toast the bread on both sides. Spread one side of each piece of toast with mayonnaise and arrange the bacon, tomatoes, and lettuce on top of two of the pieces. Season with salt and pepper and top with the other pieces of toast. Cut into quarters and serve hot or cold.

4 Canadian bacon slices
4 slices of whole-wheat bread or multigrain bread
¼ cup mayonnaise
4 tomatoes, halved
about 8 baby lettuce leaves
salt and pepper

Serves **2**
Prep time **5 minutes**
Cooking time **10 minutes**

AFFORDABILITY 1

# SPICED
## MACKEREL FILLETS

2 tablespoons olive oil
1 tablespoon smoked paprika
1 teaspoon cayenne pepper
4 mackerel, scaled, filleted, and
   pin-boned
2 limes, quartered
salt and pepper
arugula salad, to serve

Serves **4**
Prep time **4 minutes**
Cooking time **5-6 minutes**

**1** Mix together the oil, paprika, and cayenne pepper with a little salt and pepper. Make three shallow cuts in the skin of the mackerel and brush over the spiced oil.

**2** Put the lime quarters and mackerel on a hot barbecue or ridged grill pan, skin side down first, and cook for 4-5 minutes until the skin is crispy and the limes are charred. Turn the fish over and cook for a minute more on the other side. Serve with an arugula salad.

# BRAISED POLLOCK
## *with lentils*

**AFFORDABILITY 1**

1   Boil the lentils in plenty of water for 15 minutes or according to the package directions. Drain and set aside.

2   Meanwhile, heat 1 tablespoon oil in a large skillet, add the onion and fry for 5 minutes. Stir in the garlic and fry for an additional 2 minutes.

3   Add the lentils, rosemary or thyme, stock, and a little salt and pepper to the pan and bring to a boil.

4   Pour the mixture into a shallow, heatproof dish and arrange the fish on top. Score the tops of the tomatoes and tuck them around the fish. Drizzle over the remaining oil and bake, uncovered, in a preheated oven, 350°F, for 25 minutes or until the fish is cooked through. Serve sprinkled with the parsley.

¾ cup Puy lentils
3 tablespoons extra virgin olive oil
1 large onion, finely chopped
3 garlic cloves, sliced
several rosemary or thyme sprigs
scant 1 cup Fish Stock (see page 235)
4 chunky pieces of pollock fillet, skinned
8 small tomatoes
salt and pepper
2 tablespoons chopped flat leaf parsley, to garnish

Serves **4**
Prep time **15 minutes**
Cooking time **50 minutes**

# TUNA & PASTA BAKE

10 oz pasta shells
2 tablespoons olive oil
1 onion, finely chopped
2 red bell peppers, cored, seeded, and cubed
2 garlic cloves, crushed
1 cup cherry tomatoes, halved
1 tablespoon butter
1 cup fresh bread crumbs
1 13-oz can tuna, drained and flaked
4 oz mozzarella or Gruyère cheese, grated

Serves **4**
Prep time **5 minutes**
Cooking time **15 minutes**

**1** Cook the pasta shells in a saucepan of lightly salted boiling water for 8–10 minutes or according to the package directions until just tender.

**2** Meanwhile, heat the oil in a large skillet, add the onion, and fry gently for 3 minutes. Add the peppers and garlic and fry, stirring frequently, for 5 minutes. Stir in the tomatoes and fry for 1 minute until they are soft.

**3** Melt the butter in another pan, toss in the bread crumbs, and stir until all the bread is covered in butter.

**4** Drain the pasta, add the pepper and tomato mix to the drained pasta and then stir in the tuna. Mix together and transfer to a heatproof dish.

**5** Sprinkle the cheese and then the buttered bread crumbs over the pasta and cook under a medium broiler for 3–5 minutes until the cheese has melted and the bread crumbs are golden.

# *Spicy* **TUNA** FISHCAKES

1 Cook the potatoes in a large saucepan of lightly salted boiling water for 10 minutes or until tender. Drain well, mash, and allow to cool slightly.

2 Mix the tuna, cheese, green onions, garlic, thyme, and egg into the mashed potato. Season to taste with cayenne, salt, and pepper.

3 Divide the mixture into four and shape into thick patties. Season the flour with salt and pepper and dust the patties, then fry them in a shallow layer of vegetable oil for 5 minutes each side until crisp and golden. Serve hot with a mixed green salad and mayonnaise.

8 oz potatoes, diced
2 7-oz each cans tuna in olive oil, drained and flaked
½ cup grated cheddar cheese
4 green onions, finely chopped
1 small garlic clove, crushed
2 teaspoons dried thyme
1 medium egg, beaten
½ teaspoon cayenne pepper
½ cup all-purpose flour
salt and pepper
vegetable oil, for frying

**To serve**
mixed green salad
mayonnaise

Serves **4**
Prep time **10 minutes**
Cooking time **18 minutes**

### Ramp up reheat

Always reheat food thoroughly before you eat it. Leftover take-outs, in particular, have a serious reputation for rendering people incontinent and even hospital-bound. You should store leftovers in the refrigerator and heat thoroughly to kill any bugs that might be hiding. Don't reheat food more than once—if you haven't managed to eat it all in two sittings then you either ordered too much or it wasn't great quality in the first place.

# RED SALMON & ROASTED VEGETABLES

1 eggplant, cut into bite-size pieces
2 red bell peppers, cored, seeded, and cut into bite-size pieces
2 red onions, quartered
1 garlic clove, crushed
¼ cup olive oil
pinch of dried oregano
1 7-oz can red salmon, drained and flaked
½ cup pitted black olives
salt and pepper
basil leaves, to garnish

**1** Mix together the eggplant, bell peppers, onions, and garlic in a bowl with the oil and oregano and season well with salt and pepper.

**2** Spread out the vegetables in a single layer in a nonstick roasting pan and roast in a preheated oven, 425°F, for 25 minutes or until just cooked.

**3** Transfer the vegetables to a warm serving dish and gently toss in the salmon and olives. Garnish with basil leaves and serve warm or at room temperature.

Serves **4**
Prep time **10 minutes**
Cooking time **25 minutes**

# CREAMY TUNA & LEEK PASTA

1 Plunge the pasta into a large saucepan of lightly salted boiling water. Return to a boil and cook for 10-12 minutes or according to the package directions until just tender. Drain well and return to the pan.

2 Meanwhile, heat the oil in a skillet, add the leeks, garlic, and salt and pepper to taste and cook gently for 5 minutes.

3 Add the tuna and cook, stirring, for 1 minute. Add the wine, bring to a boil, and boil until reduced by half. Stir in the cream and heat through for 2-3 minutes.

4 Add the tuna sauce to the pasta with the parsley and stir over a medium heat for 1 minute. Serve immediately with an arugula salad.

13 oz dried penne
2 tablespoons extra virgin olive oil
2 leeks, sliced
2 large garlic cloves, sliced
2 7-oz each cans tuna in olive oil, drained and flaked
2/3 cup dry white wine
2/3 cup whipping cream
2 tablespoons chopped parsley
salt and pepper
arugula salad, to serve

Serves **4**
Prep time **10 minutes**
Cooking time **12 minutes**

AFFORDABILITY
1

# KEDGEREE

7 oz smoked haddock
scant 1 cup milk
1 bay leaf
2 teaspoons vegetable oil
1 small onion, chopped
½ cup basmati rice
½ teaspoon curry powder
2 hard-cooked eggs, roughly
  chopped
1 tablespoon chopped parsley

Serves **2**
Prep time **10 minutes**
Cooking time **15 minutes**

1 Put the haddock in a small saucepan with the milk and bay leaf, simmer for 3 minutes or until just cooked and remove the fish, reserving the milk. Flake the fish and set aside.

2 Heat the oil in a skillet, add the onion, and fry for 3 minutes. Add the rice and curry powder, stir and fry for another minute.

3 Make up the reserved milk to 1 cup with water and pour it over the rice. Cover and cook for 12 minutes until the rice is cooked and fluffy. Add the remaining ingredients and the flaked haddock, stir to combine, and serve.

# MUSHROOM STROGANOFF

**AFFORDABILITY 1**

1 Melt the butter with the oil in a large skillet, add the onion and garlic and cook until soft and starting to brown.

2 Add the mushrooms to the pan and cook until soft and starting to brown. Stir in the mustard and sour cream and just heat through. Season to taste with salt and pepper, then serve immediately, garnished with the chopped parsley.

1 tablespoon butter
2 tablespoons olive oil
1 onion, thinly sliced
4 garlic cloves, finely chopped
6 cups sliced brown mushrooms
   (1 lb)
2 tablespoons whole-grain
   mustard
1 cup sour cream
salt and pepper
3 tablespoons chopped parsley, to
   garnish

Serves **4**
Prep time **10 minutes**
Cooking time **10 minutes**

# CORN
## *&* PEPPER
# *Frittata*

AFFORDABILITY
1

2 tablespoons olive oil
4 green onions, thinly sliced
1 7-oz can corn, drained
1 cup ready-roasted red bell
   peppers in oil, drained and cut
   into strips
4 eggs, lightly beaten
1 cup grated sharp cheddar cheese
small handful of chives, finely
   chopped
salt and pepper

**To serve**
green salad
crusty bread

Serves **4**
Prep time **10 minutes**
Cooking time **10 minutes**

1 Heat the oil in a skillet with a flameproof handle, add the green onions, corn, and bell peppers, and cook for 30 seconds.

2 Add the eggs, cheese, and chives, season to taste with salt and pepper, and cook over a medium heat for 4–5 minutes until the base is set. Remove from the stove and place under a preheated broiler and cook for 3–4 minutes or until golden and set.

3 Cut into wedges and serve immediately with a green salad and crusty bread.

# CAULIFLOWER CHEESE

1 large cauliflower, divided into
    florets
2 tablespoons butter
¼ cup all-purpose flour
1¼ cups milk
1 cup grated cheddar cheese
1 teaspoon Dijon mustard
1 tablespoon fresh bread crumbs
salt and pepper
4 broiled Canadian bacon slices,
    cut into strips, to garnish

Serves **4**
Prep time **10 minutes**
Cooking time **15 minutes**

**1** Steam the cauliflower over a pan of lightly salted boiling water for about 12 minutes until tender. Drain and transfer to a heatproof dish.

**2** Meanwhile, melt the butter in a heavy saucepan, stir in the flour and cook for 1 minute. Slowly stir in the milk, then two-thirds of the cheddar and heat. Stir constantly, until the sauce has thickened. Season with mustard, salt, and pepper.

**3** Pour the sauce over the cauliflower, sprinkle with the remaining cheese and sprinkle the bread crumbs over the top. Cook under a medium broiler until the top is golden brown. Garnish with bacon strips.

AFFORDABILITY **1**

# INDIVIDUAL MAC & CHEESE

1 Cook the macaroni in a large saucepan of lightly salted boiling water for 10-12 minutes or according to the package directions until just tender. Drain and place in a large bowl.

2 Meanwhile, dry-fry the bacon in a small skillet until browned but not crisp. Add the garlic, fry for 1 minute and then add the cream and milk and season with a little nutmeg. Bring just to boiling point.

3 Stir in 1 cup of the cheese and all the basil, remove from the heat, and stir until the cheese melts. Season to taste with salt and pepper and stir into the macaroni.

4 Spoon into individual gratin dishes, top with the remaining cheese, and bake in a preheated oven, 450°F, for 10 minutes, until golden.

8 oz macaroni
4 Canadian bacon slices, diced
1 garlic clove, crushed
2/3 cup light cream
2/3 cup milk
pinch of grated nutmeg
1½ cups grated hard cheese, such as cheddar or Gruyère
¼ cup chopped basil
salt and pepper

Serves **4**
Prep time **5 minutes**
Cooking time **20 minutes**

3 tablespoons sunflower oil
10 oz firm tofu, cubed
1 onion, sliced
2 carrots, sliced
5 oz broccoli, broken into small
   florets and stalks sliced
1 red bell pepper, cored, seeded,
   and sliced
1 large zucchini, sliced
5 oz sugar snap peas
2 tablespoons soy sauce
2 tablespoons sweet chili sauce

**To garnish**
chopped red chiles
Thai or ordinary basil leaves

Serves **4**
Prep time **10 minutes**
Cooking time **7 minutes**

AFFORDABILITY
1

# **VEGETABLE** & TOFU
# STIR-FRY

**1** Heat 1 tablespoon of the oil in a wok or large skillet until it starts to smoke, add the tofu, and stir-fry over a high heat for 2 minutes until golden. Remove from the pan with a slotted spoon.

**2** Heat the remaining oil in the pan, add the onion and carrots and stir-fry for 1½ minutes. Add the broccoli and bell pepper and stir-fry for 1 minute, then add the zucchini and sugar snap peas and stir-fry for 1 minute.

**3** Mix the soy and chili sauces with ½ cup water and add to the pan with the tofu. Cook for 1 minute. Serve in bowls, garnished with chopped red chiles and basil leaves.

AFFORDABILITY

# STIR-FRIED VEGETABLE *Noodles*

1 Cook the noodles in a large saucepan of lightly salted boiling water for about 4 minutes or until just tender. Drain.

2 Heat the oil in a large skillet or wok, add the green onions and carrots and stir-fry for 3 minutes. Add the garlic, red pepper flakes, snow peas, and mushrooms and stir-fry for 2 minutes. Add the Chinese cabbage leaves and stir-fry for 1 minute.

3 Add the drained noodles to the pan with the soy sauce and hoisin sauce. Stir-fry over a gentle heat for 2 minutes until heated through and serve immediately.

8 oz egg noodles
¼ cup peanut oil
1 bunch of green onions, sliced
2 carrots, thinly sliced
2 garlic cloves, crushed
¼ teaspoon dried red pepper flakes
4 oz snow peas
4 oz shiitake mushrooms, halved
3 Chinese cabbage leaves, shredded
2 tablespoons light soy sauce
3 tablespoons hoisin sauce

Serves **4**
Prep time **10 minutes**
Cooking time **12 minutes**

# Herb Omelet
## WITH MUSTARD
# MUSHROOMS

IF YOU PREFER, COOK HALF THE EGG MIXTURE AT A TIME TO MAKE TWO SMALLER OMELETS.

1 tablespoon whole-grain mustard
4 tablespoons butter, softened
4 flat mushrooms
2 tablespoons chopped mixed
   herbs (such as chives, parsley,
   and tarragon)
4 eggs
salt and pepper

Serves **2**
Prep time **5 minutes**
Cooking time **10 minutes**

**1** Beat the mustard into 3 tablespoons butter and spread over the undersides of the mushrooms. Place on a foil-lined broiler pan and broil for 5-6 minutes until golden and tender. Remove and keep warm.

**2** Meanwhile, beat the herbs into the eggs and season to taste with salt and pepper.

**3** Melt the remaining butter in an omelet pan or nonstick skillet, swirl in the egg mixture and cook until almost set. Carefully slide and flip over onto a warmed plate, add the mushrooms, and serve.

## Bottle it up

It's worth keeping a few glass jars and lids in the kitchen. They're handy for mixing up salad dressings or sauces. Alternatively, if you're going for a hippy chick look for your next gathering, pop a tea light or small bunch of flowers (or pretty weeds, if gardening isn't your forte) inside for table decorations.

AFFORDABILITY
**1**

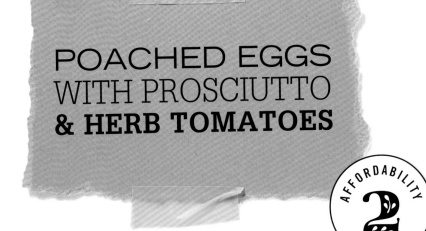

# POACHED EGGS
## WITH PROSCIUTTO
## & HERB TOMATOES

*THIS IS A HEALTHIER VERSION OF THE TRADITIONAL "FRY-UP."*

1 Halve the tomatoes and place them, cut side up, on a foil-lined broiler pan. Mix the basil with 2 tablespoons oil and drizzle over the tomatoes. Season well with salt and pepper. Cook under a preheated broiler for 6-7 minutes until softened. Remove and keep warm.

2 Meanwhile, heat the remaining oil in a skillet and fry the prosciutto until crisp. Drain on paper towels and keep warm.

3 Poach the eggs in gently simmering water or an egg poacher for 3-4 minutes. Serve on buttered toasted English muffins with the prosciutto and broiled tomatoes.

4 ripe tomatoes
2 tablespoons chopped basil
¼ cup extra virgin olive oil
4 slices of prosciutto
4 large eggs
salt and pepper
hot buttered English muffins, to serve

Serves **4**
Prep time **5 minutes**
Cooking time **10-12 minutes**

# POTATO TORTILLA

⅔ cup extra virgin olive oil
1½ lb waxy potatoes, thinly sliced
1 onion, chopped
1 red bell pepper, cored, seeded,
   and sliced
1 bell green pepper, cored, seeded,
   and sliced
5 eggs, beaten
salt and pepper

Serves **6**
Prep time **10 minutes**
Cooking time **30-35 minutes**

1 Heat all but 2 tablespoons of the oil in a large nonstick skillet and fry the potatoes, onion, and peppers, stirring frequently, for 15 minutes, until all the vegetables are golden and tender.

2 Mix the potato mixture with the eggs in a large bowl and season well with salt and pepper. Set aside for 15 minutes. Clean the skillet.

3 Heat the remaining oil in the clean pan and tip in the tortilla mixture. Cook over a low heat for 10 minutes, until almost cooked through. Carefully slide the tortilla onto a large plate, invert the skillet over the tortilla and then flip it back into the skillet.

4 Return the pan to the heat and cook the tortilla for 5 minutes more, or until it is cooked on both sides. Allow to cool, then serve at room temperature, cut into wedges.

# CANNELLINI BEANS ON TOAST

1 Heat the oil in a saucepan, add the onion and celery, and fry for 5 minutes until golden. Blend the cornstarch with 2 tablespoons water and add to the pan with the remaining ingredients.

2 Bring to a boil, reduce the heat slightly and season to taste with salt and pepper. Cook, uncovered, for about 20 minutes, stirring frequently, until the mixture is thick and pulpy. Pile on toast to serve.

2 tablespoons peanut or vegetable oil
1 onion, chopped
1 celery stick, thinly sliced
1 teaspoon cornstarch
1 14-oz can cannellini beans
1 8-oz can diced tomatoes
1¼ cups Vegetable Stock (see page 235)
1 tablespoon whole-grain mustard
1 tablespoon molasses
1 tablespoon ketchup
1 tablespoon Worcestershire sauce
salt and pepper
toasted chunky bread, to serve

Serves **2-3**
Prep time **5 minutes**
Cooking time **25 minutes**

# RATATOUILLE

½ cup olive oil

2 large eggplants, quartered lengthwise and cut into ½-inch slices

2 zucchini, cut into ½-inch slices

2 large red bell peppers, cored, seeded, and cut into squares

1 large yellow bell pepper, cored, seeded, and cut into squares

2 large onions, thinly sliced

3 large garlic cloves, crushed

2 tablespoons tomato paste

1 13-oz can plum tomatoes

12 basil leaves, chopped

1 tablespoon finely chopped marjoram or oregano

1 teaspoon finely chopped thyme

1 tablespoon paprika

2-4 tablespoons finely chopped parsley

salt and pepper

Serves **8**
Prep time **10 minutes**
Cooking time **30 minutes**

1 Heat half the oil in a roasting pan in a preheated oven, 425°F. Add the eggplants, zucchini, and peppers and toss in the hot oil, return to the oven, and roast for about 30 minutes or until tender.

2 Meanwhile, heat the remaining oil in a deep saucepan, add the onions and garlic and cook over a medium heat for 3-5 minutes until softened but not browned. Add the tomato paste, plum tomatoes, herbs, and paprika and season to taste with salt and pepper. Stir to combine, then cook for 10-15 minutes until the mixture is thick and syrupy.

3 Use a slotted spoon to transfer the vegetables from the roasting pan to the tomato mixture. Gently stir to combine, then add the parsley and adjust the seasoning if necessary. Serve hot or cold with crusty bread or as an accompaniment to meats or poultry.

# POTATO WEDGES & PEPPERS WITH YOGURT DIP

1 Cut the potato into eight wedges. Bring a saucepan of lightly salted water to a boil, add the potato wedges and cook for 5 minutes. Drain the wedges thoroughly and put them in a bowl with the bell pepper slices and oil. Toss well to mix. Sprinkle with paprika and rock salt to taste.

2 Put the potato wedges and pepper slices on a baking sheet and cook under a preheated hot broiler, turning occasionally, for 6-8 minutes until lightly browned and tender.

3 Meanwhile, make the yogurt dip. In a bowl mix together all the ingredients and season to taste with salt and pepper.

4 Serve the potato wedges and pepper slices hot with the yogurt dip.

1 potato, about 6 oz, scrubbed
1 red bell pepper, cored, seeded, and sliced
1 teaspoon olive oil
paprika
rock salt

**Yogurt dip**
3 tablespoons Greek-style yogurt
1 tablespoon chopped parsley
2 green onions, chopped
1 garlic clove, crushed (optional)
salt and pepper

Serves **2**
Prep time **15 minutes**
Cooking time **15 minutes**

### Bag it up

Next time you go to the supermarket, stock up on a few packs of freezer bags. They take up less storage space than plastic containers and they're ideal for freezing leftover portions of sauces, curries, etc. Use a marker pen to stake your claim to your culinary masterpieces and lay them flat in the freezer drawer.

# EAT
## HEALTHY

EGGPLANT & POTATO
CAKES

CHICKPEAS WITH CHORIZO

THREE PEPPER SALAD

DUCK TACOS

**Nutrient analysis per serving**

| 1549 kJ | 371 kcal | energy |
|---|---|---|
| | 33.3 g | protein |
| | 15.2 g | carbohydrate |
| | 7.6 g | sugars |
| | 20.0 g | fat |
| | 4.1 g | saturates |
| | 3.3 g | fiber |
| | 268 mg | sodium |

# CHICKEN & CASHEW NUTS
# WITH VEGETABLES

1 cup Chicken Stock (see page 234)
13 oz boneless, skinless chicken breast, cubed
2 tablespoons store-bought yellow bean sauce
1 cup sliced carrots (7 oz)
1 cup sliced bamboo shoots (7 oz)
1½ cups cashew nuts, toasted
1 green onion, shredded

**Cornstarch paste**
1 teaspoon cornstarch
2 tablespoons water or stock

Serves **4**
Prep time **15 minutes**
Cooking time **15 minutes**

1 Put the stock in a saucepan and bring to a boil. Add the chicken meat and bring the liquid back to boil, stirring. Lower the heat and cook for 5 minutes. Remove the chicken with a slotted spoon and set aside.

2 Add the yellow bean sauce and cook for a couple of minutes. Add the carrots and bamboo shoots and cook for another couple of minutes.

3 Make the cornstarch paste. Mix the cornstarch with the water or stock to make a smooth, lump-free paste.

4 Return the chicken to the pan, bring the sauce back to a boil and thicken with the cornstarch paste. Stir in the cashew nuts and green onion just before serving. Serve with rice, if desired.

# CHICKEN, COUSCOUS & ONIONS

1 Put the chicken in a large saucepan, add 3 cups water and bring slowly to a boil. Add the bouquet garni, onion, garlic, saffron, and 1¼ teaspoons of salt. Reduce the heat, cover, and simmer for 50-60 minutes until the chicken is tender. Add the ginger and pepper 5 minutes before the end of cooking.

2 Meanwhile, put the couscous in a bowl and cover it with water. Rake it through with your fingers, then drain and immediately spread it evenly over a large tray. Rake the grains with your fingers a few times to aerate them, then leave for 20-30 minutes until the water is absorbed and the couscous is relatively dry.

3 Rub the couscous gently between your palms, letting it fall back into the tray, to break down any lumps. Sprinkle with the remaining salt, drizzle over 1 tablespoon of the oil, and rake through the grains again.

4 Ladle 1¼ cups stock from the large pan into a small pan and bring to a rapid boil, turn off the heat, and add the couscous. Cover and leave until the stock has been absorbed.

5 Heat the remaining oil in a pan, add the onions, and fry gently until lightly golden. Ladle a scant cup of stock into a small bowl. Pour a little of this stock over the onions and cook until reduced. Repeat until all the stock has been added and reduced. As the onions soften, increase the heat.

6 Add the raisins, cinnamon, and nutmeg, then the honey and let caramelize for 5-10 minutes. Stir in the flower water or rose water, if using, and turn off the heat.

7 Transfer the couscous to a serving dish and top with the onions. Serve the chicken and stock separately.

1 small chicken, cut into 6-8 pieces
bouquet garni (1 cinnamon stick, 1 bay leaf, 1 cardamom pod, tied together with string)
1 onion, finely chopped
3 garlic cloves, crushed
generous pinch of saffron threads
1½ teaspoons salt
½ teaspoon ground ginger
¼ teaspoon ground black pepper
1½ cups couscous
2 tablespoons extra virgin olive oil
2 cups sliced onions (1 lb)
½ cup raisins
½ teaspoon ground cinnamon
small pinch of grated nutmeg
1-2 tablespoons honey
scant ½ tablespoon orange flower water or rose water (optional)

Serves **4-6**
Prep time **1 hour**
Cooking time **1½ hours**

**Nutrient analysis per serving**

| 3256 kJ | 780 kcal | energy |
|---|---|---|
| | 46 g | protein |
| | 66 g | carbohydrate |
| | 32 g | sugars |
| | 39 g | fat |
| | 9 g | saturates |
| | 3 g | fiber |
| | 0.7 g | sodium |

# DUCK
## TACOS

3½-lb hot roasted duck
16 soft corn tortillas
1 onion, finely chopped
8 green chiles, chopped (seeded
  for a milder taste)
½ cup finely chopped cilantro
salt
finely chopped tomato, to garnish
  (optional)
salsa of your choice, to serve

Serves **4**
Prep time **20 minutes**
Cooking time **6-8 minutes**

**1** Shred the hot roasted duck meat, discarding any fat, and keep warm.

**2** Preheat a large, dry, heavy skillet over a medium heat, warm each side of the tortillas, two or three at a time, for about 30 seconds in the hot pan until soft. Transfer to a basket and cover with a clean dish towel.

**3** Put about ¾ oz of shredded duck on top of one warm tortilla, sprinkle with some of the onion, chiles, and cilantro on top, season with salt to taste, roll up, and place on a warm platter. Cover with the clean dish towel. Repeat with the remaining ingredients.

**4** Serve immediately with your favorite salsa and garnish with chopped tomato, if desired.

## Healthy tip

DUCK CAN BE HIGH IN FAT,
SO ALWAYS REMOVE THE SKIN
AND AS MUCH FAT AS
POSSIBLE TO MAKE THIS
NUTRITIOUS DISH HEALTHIER.

### Nutrient analysis per serving

| | | |
|---|---|---|
| 3430 kJ | 816 kcal | energy |
| | 54 g | protein |
| | 93 g | carbohydrate |
| | 2 g | sugars |
| | 25 g | fat |
| | 4 g | saturates |
| | 5 g | fiber |
| | 570 mg | sodium |

# SAVORY MEATBALLS

10 oz ground pork
3 garlic cloves, crushed
½ cup dried white bread crumbs
1 teaspoon ground cumin
1 teaspoon ground coriander
1 teaspoon grated nutmeg
1 teaspoon ground cinnamon
2 tablespoons olive oil
salt and pepper

**Sauce**
1 tablespoon olive oil
1 small onion, finely chopped
1 garlic clove, crushed
1 14½-oz can diced tomatoes
1 teaspoon unrefined sugar
1 teaspoon mild paprika
⅔ cup fresh or frozen peas

Makes **about 30**
Prep time **20 minutes, plus chilling**
Cooking time **40-50 minutes**

**1** Put the ground meat, garlic, bread crumbs, and spices in a bowl. Season to taste with salt and pepper. Use your fingers to mix thoroughly. Cover and chill in the refrigerator for 1 hour.

**2** Meanwhile, make the sauce. Heat the oil in a large skillet, cook the onion and garlic over a medium heat, stirring frequently, for 5-6 minutes. Stir in the tomatoes, sugar, and paprika, bring to a boil. Reduce the heat, cover, and simmer gently, stirring occasionally, for 25-30 minutes. Add the peas, season to taste with salt and pepper, and cook for 2-3 minutes.

**3** Shape walnut-size pieces of the meat mixture into balls. Heat half the oil in a nonstick skillet and cook half the meatballs over a medium heat, stirring, for 2-3 minutes until browned all over. Remove with a slotted spoon and drain on paper towels. Repeat with the remaining oil and meatballs.

**4** Add the meatballs to the sauce over a medium heat, stir to coat evenly, then simmer gently for 5-6 minutes. Serve hot.

| Nutrient analysis per serving | |
|---|---|
| 1122 kJ   266 kcal | energy |
| 20 g | protein |
| 15 g | carbohydrate |
| 6 g | sugars |
| 15 g | fat |
| 3 g | saturates |
| 3 g | fiber |
| 164 mg | sodium |

# BROILED
# PORK STEAKS WITH SAGE

1 Using a sharp knife, cut a horizontal pocket through the center of each pork steak.

2 Mix together the garlic, sage, and oil and rub this mixture all over the outside and inside of the pork steaks. Place in a dish, cover, and allow to marinate in the refrigerator for at least 30 minutes or overnight.

3 Season the outside and inside of the pork steaks with salt and pepper and place them on a foil-lined baking sheet. Cook under a preheated hot broiler, about 4 inches from the heat, for 5 minutes. Turn over the steaks and cook for 5 minutes more or until cooked through and golden.

4 pork loin steaks, about 7 oz each
2 garlic cloves, finely chopped
1½ tablespoons finely chopped
  sage
1 teaspoon olive oil
salt and pepper

Serves **4**
Prep time **15 minutes, plus marinating**
Cooking time **10 minutes**

## Healthy tip

PORK USED TO BE A VERY FATTY MEAT, BUT TODAY PIGS ARE BRED TO BE MUCH LEANER. THERE IS STILL A CERTAIN AMOUNT OF INVISIBLE FAT INCORPORATED IN THE LEAN MEAT, WHICH HELPS GIVE PORK ITS TEXTURE AND FLAVOR, SO TRIM ANY VISIBLE FAT OFF TO KEEP THE MEAT AS LEAN AS POSSIBLE.

### Nutrient analysis per serving

| 1280 kJ | 306 kcal | energy |
|---|---|---|
| | 42 g | protein |
| | 1 g | carbohydrate |
| | 0 g | sugars |
| | 15 g | fat |
| | 5 g | saturates |
| | 0 g | fiber |
| | 74 mg | sodium |

AFFORDABILITY
1

# CHICKPEAS
## WITH CHORIZO

AFFORDABILITY
1

2 tablespoons olive oil
1 red onion, finely chopped
2 garlic cloves, crushed
7 oz chorizo sausage, cut into
½-inch dice
2 ripe tomatoes, deseeded and
finely chopped
3 tablespoons chopped flat leaf
parsley
2 13-oz each cans chickpeas in
water, rinsed and drained
salt and pepper

Serves **4**
Prep time **10 minutes**
Cooking time **10 minutes**

1 Heat the oil in a large, nonstick skillet, add the onion, garlic, and chorizo and cook over a medium-high heat, stirring frequently, for 4-5 minutes.

2 Add the tomatoes, parsley, and chickpeas to the pan and cook, stirring frequently, for 4-5 minutes until heated through. Season to taste with salt and pepper and serve immediately or allow to cool to room temperature.

## Healthy tip

CHICKPEAS ARE NOT ONLY A GREAT SOURCE OF DIETARY FIBER, THEY ALSO CONTAIN IRON, WHICH IS ESSENTIAL FOR HEALTHY BLOOD. THE VITAMIN C FROM THE TOMATOES IN THIS DISH WILL HELP IN THE ABSORPTION OF THE IRON.

### Nutrient analysis per serving

| 1737 kJ   415 kcal | energy |
|---|---|
| 24 g | protein |
| 36 g | carbohydrate |
| 7 g | sugars |
| 21 g | fat |
| 6 g | saturates |
| 10 g | fiber |
| 300 mg | sodium |

# ROASTED SEA BASS
# WITH **POTATOES**
## & WILD MUSHROOMS

IF FRESH WILD MUSHROOMS ARE NOT AVAILABLE, USE A COMBINATION OF DRIED PORCINI AND CULTIVATED MUSHROOMS, REDUCING THE SOAKING LIQUID FROM THE PORCINI AND ADDING IT TO THE POTATOES WITH THE MUSHROOMS.

1¾ lb potatoes, peeled
2 garlic cloves, thinly sliced
3 tablespoons olive oil
8 oz mixed wild mushrooms, sliced if large
4 sea bass fillets, about 6 oz each
½ tablespoon chopped flat leaf parsley
extra virgin olive oil, for drizzling
salt and pepper

Serves **4**
Prep time **15 minutes**
Cooking time **35-40 minutes**

1 Cut the potatoes into slices about ½ inch thick and put them in a large roasting pan lined with waxed paper. Stir in half the garlic and 2 tablespoons olive oil and season with salt and pepper. Spread out the potatoes in a single layer and roast in a preheated oven, 475°F, for 18-20 minutes or until cooked through and golden.

2 Meanwhile, heat ½ tablespoon of the remaining olive oil in a skillet over a high heat, add the mushrooms and the remaining garlic and cook, stirring frequently, until just tender. Season with salt and pepper.

3 Stir the cooked mushrooms into the roasted potatoes. Season the sea bass fillets and place them, skin side up, on top of the potatoes. Sprinkle with the parsley and drizzle the fish with the remaining olive oil. Roast for 10-12 minutes until the fish is cooked through. Serve immediately with a drizzle of extra virgin olive oil.

## Healthy tip

SEA BASS IS A LOW-FAT FISH THAT PROVIDES USEFUL AMOUNTS OF VITAMIN A AND SELENIUM (THOUGHT TO AID IN THE PREVENTION OF CANCER).

### Nutrient analysis per serving

| 1839 kJ | 438 kcal | energy |
|---|---|---|
| | 40 g | protein |
| | 38 g | carbohydrate |
| | 2 g | sugars |
| | 15 g | fat |
| | 2 g | saturates |
| | 5 g | fiber |
| | 140 mg | sodium |

# BENGALI-STYLE
# MUSTARD FISH

**1** Use a mortar and pestle to crush the turmeric, chili powder, whole-grain mustard, and black mustard seeds until fairly well combined. Add the oil and lime juice and season well. Stir to mix thoroughly.

**2** Line a baking sheet with nonstick parchment paper and put the fish fillets on the baking sheet. Spread the mustard mixture over the fish and cook in a preheated oven, 400°F, for 15–20 minutes or until cooked through. Remove from the oven and serve immediately, garnished with chopped cilantro.

1 teaspoon turmeric
1 teaspoon chili powder
2 tablespoons whole-grain mustard
2 teaspoons black mustard seeds
2 tablespoons sunflower oil
juice of 1 lime
salt
4 thick halibut or cod fillets, each about 8 oz, skinned
chopped cilantro leaves, to garnish

Serves **4**
Prep time **10 minutes**
Cooking time **15–20 minutes**

## Something fishy

Fish is ultra-healthy and easy to cook, but it doesn't often feature on student dinner menus. For a fuss-free fish supper drizzle some olive oil into a large square of kitchen foil, place the fish fillet on top and add a lemon slice and any herbs you have lying around. Make the foil into a loose, sealed parcel around the fish and cook for 12–15 minutes (depending on size). The fish will be moist and the kitchen won't smell. Perfect!

AFFORDABILITY **3**

### Nutrient analysis per serving

| 958 kJ | 228 kcal | energy |
|---|---|---|
| | 32 g | protein |
| | 1 g | carbohydrate |
| | 0 g | sugars |
| | 11 g | fat |
| | 1 g | saturates |
| | 0 g | fiber |
| | 274 mg | sodium |

# TREAT YOUR
# BODY
## LIKE A TEMPLE

◇◇◇◇◇◇◇◇◇◇◇◇◇◇◇◇◇◇◇◇◇◇◇◇◇◇◇◇◇◇◇◇◇◇◇◇◇◇◇◇◇◇◇◇◇◇◇◇◇◇◇◇◇◇◇◇

If you think you can get your five a day from a steady diet of vodka and orange you're going to have to re-think your eating habits. That's not to say that vodka has to be banished entirely – you just need to shuffle the proportions to make way for healthy additions. It is possible to eat well and to still have a few cents left over for happy hour.

## IRON IT OUT

You need iron to keep your blood bubbling away happily. If you're a carnivore you'll have no problems stocking up. However, if you shy away from steak, you should nibble nuts, dried fruit, and plenty of green vegetables.

## FORTY WINKS

Mid-week all nighters are inevitable but try to squeez in a regular 8 hours' sl

| Suggestions for your five a day | Portion size |
|---|---|
| Orange juice with breakfast | 5-oz glass |
| Chopped fruit on cereal | a handful of grapes or 7 strawberries |
| Fruit snack | apple, banana, orange, pear, etc |
| Salad snack | 1 tomato, 3 celery sticks, or a handful of cherry tomatoes |
| Dried fruit | 1 tablespoon |
| Vegetable portion | 2 broccoli florets, 3 tablespoons cooked peas, corn, or carrots |

## FIGHTING FIT

Protein helps your body to heal itself and grow so it should be muscling in on most of your meals. Chicken, eggs, dairy produce, fish, and grains are all good sources, so it shouldn't be too taxing to find ways of putting protein on your plate.

## ENERGY FOOD

As well as plenty of fruit and vegetables, you should try to include "good" carbohydrates in your diet. By "good" we're talking about the slow burners that will release energy gradually and keep you feeling full. Whole-wheat or multigrain bread, pasta, rice, and potatoes are all good, cheap sources of carbohydrates, and these should have a big presence on the dinner table.

## STRETCH YOUR LEGS

Running for a lecture after you've overslept or bed-hopping your way around the campus might supply sporadic bouts of exercise, but you really should include some kind of regular sporting activity in your weekly schedule. Let's face it: if you can't find the time for a quick game of football or a step class when you're at college then you never will.

The choices you make now regarding your diet and lifestyle can have long-term implications. At the risk of sounding like your mom, you need to make sure you eat properly and look after yourself. That means eating regular, healthy meals (rather than replacing solid food with a liquid diet) and getting fresh air and exercise. Student dormitories are worse than a medieval city for the rapid spread of every contagious illness known to mankind, and your best chance of avoiding flu, endless colds, and other nasty bugs related to communal living is to boost your immune system with a balanced diet.

# TRADITIONAL
## FISH & POTATO
# STEW

1 lb 10 oz tuna fillets, cut into large
 bite-size pieces
¼ cup olive oil
2 red onions, halved and thinly
 sliced
4 garlic cloves, thinly sliced
3 ripe tomatoes, skinned, seeded,
 and chopped
2 bay leaves
1 red bell pepper, cored, seeded,
 and diced
1 tablespoon mild paprika
1¼ lb potatoes, peeled and cut into
 large bite-size pieces
salt and pepper

**To garnish**
chopped flat leaf parsley
capers

Serves **4**
Prep time **15 minutes**
Cooking time **40-45 minutes**

**1** Arrange the tuna in a shallow bowl in a single layer and
season to taste with salt and pepper. Cover and set aside.

**2** Heat the oil in a saucepan, add the onions and garlic,
and cook over a medium heat, stirring frequently, for
8-10 minutes until soft.

**3** Add the tomatoes, bay leaves, bell pepper, paprika, and
potatoes and stir to mix well. Add enough water to just
cover all the ingredients and bring to a boil. Reduce the heat
and simmer gently for 25-30 minutes or until the potatoes are
tender. Add the fish, return to a boil, and cook for 4-5 minutes.

**4** Taste and adjust the seasoning if necessary and serve
ladled into warmed shallow bowls and garnished with
chopped parsley and capers.

## Healthy tip

TUNA IS AN EXCELLENT, LOW-FAT
SOURCE OF PROTEIN. THE
COMBINATION OF TUNA WITH
POTATOES, TOMATOES, AND
ONIONS MAKES THIS A
PARTICULARLY NUTRITIOUS DISH.

### Nutrient analysis per serving

| 2299 kJ | 547 kcal | energy |
|---|---|---|
| | 53 g | protein |
| | 39 g | carbohydrate |
| | 11 g | sugars |
| | 21 g | fat |
| | 4 g | saturates |
| | 6 g | fiber |
| | 119 mg | sodium |

# *Pumpkin* CURRY

**1** Put the pumpkin or butternut squash in a saucepan with the turmeric, paprika, and 3 cups water. Bring to a boil and simmer gently for 6–8 minutes or until tender.

**2** Grind half the coconut in a spice mill or a mortar and pestle with the cumin seeds. Stir this into the pumpkin mixture and stir and cook for 2–3 minutes. Remove from the heat.

**3** Heat the oil in a small, nonstick skillet, add the mustard seeds, curry leaves, and red chiles, stir, and cook over a high heat for 1–2 minutes. Tip this mixture over the pumpkin curry. Season to taste and serve sprinkled with the remaining grated coconut.

4 cups pumpkin or butternut squash, cut into 1-inch cubes (1 lb)
1 teaspoon turmeric
1 teaspoon smoked paprika
2½ cups freshly grated coconut
1 teaspoon cumin seeds
1 tablespoon sunflower oil
1 teaspoon black mustard seeds
8–10 curry leaves
2 small red chiles, split in half lengthwise
salt and pepper

Serves **4**
Prep time **10 minutes**
Cooking time **10–13 minutes**

AFFORDABILITY
**1**

## Nutrient analysis per serving

| 976 kJ | 236 kcal | energy |
|---|---|---|
| | 3 g | protein |
| | 7 g | carbohydrate |
| | 4 g | sugars |
| | 22 g | fat |
| | 16 g | saturates |
| | 7 g | fiber |
| | 12 mg | sodium |

### Healthy tip

ORANGE-FLESHED VEGETABLES ARE AN EXCELLENT SOURCE OF THE IMMUNE-BOOSTING NUTRIENT BETA-CAROTENE.

# CHICKPEA CURRY

1 tablespoon sunflower oil
2 garlic cloves, crushed
1 teaspoon finely grated fresh ginger root
2 tablespoons medium or hot curry powder
1 14½-oz can diced tomatoes
1 teaspoon grated jaggery or palm sugar
2 13-oz each cans chickpeas, rinsed and drained
salt
low-fat yogurt, to drizzle
small handful of chopped cilantro leaves, to garnish

**1** Heat the oil in a large, nonstick wok or skillet, add the garlic and ginger, and stir-fry for 30 seconds. Add the curry powder, stir and cook for 1 minute, then add the chopped tomatoes and jaggery or palm sugar. Bring the mixture to a boil, cover, reduce the heat and cook over a medium heat for 10-12 minutes.

**2** Stir in the chickpeas and mix well. Cook over a medium heat for 3-4 minutes. Season, remove from the heat.

**3** Drizzle with low-fat yogurt and sprinkle over chopped cilantro before serving.

Serves **4**
Prep time **10 minutes**
Cooking time **13-15 minutes**

### Nutrient analysis per serving

| 1232 kJ | 292 kcal | energy |
|---|---|---|
| | 16 g | protein |
| | 39 g | carbohydrate |
| | 5 g | sugars |
| | 9 g | fat |
| | 1 g | saturates |
| | 1 g | fiber |
| | 503 mg | sodium |

### Healthy tip

LEGUMES SUCH AS CHICKPEAS CONTAIN USEFUL AMOUNTS OF B VITAMINS, IRON, CALCIUM, AND FIBER. THEY ARE ALSO A GOOD SOURCE OF COMPLEX CARBOHYDRATES, WHICH PROVIDE A STEADY STREAM OF ENERGY.

# HUEVOS RANCHEROS

1 Make the sauce. Put the tomatoes, onion, garlic, and chiles in a blender or food processor and blend until the mixture is a fairly smooth texture.

2 Heat the oil in a saucepan set over a medium heat, add the tomato mixture and simmer, stirring constantly, for about 10 minutes or until cooked. Add salt to taste and keep warm until required.

3 Preheat a large, dry, heavy skillet over a medium heat. Brush the tortillas with oil and warm each side of two tortillas at a time in the hot pan for about 30 seconds until soft. Cover with kitchen foil to keep warm.

4 Preheat a dry, nonstick skillet over a medium heat. Break the eggs, two at a time, into the pan and cook over a low heat until the whites have set.

5 Put one tortilla on each plate and place two cooked eggs on top. Spoon the sauce generously over the whites of the eggs, leaving the yolks exposed, and serve immediately with flat leaf parsley sprinkled over the top, if desired.

4 soft corn tortillas
vegetable oil, for brushing
8 large eggs

**Ranchera sauce**
4 ripe tomatoes
½ onion, coarsely chopped
1 garlic clove, coarsely chopped
4 green chiles, coarsely chopped
   (seeded for a milder taste)
1 tablespoon vegetable oil
salt
chopped flat leaf parsley, to
   garnish (optional)

Serves **4**
Prep time **15 minutes**
Cooking time **15-20 minutes**

## Nutrient analysis per serving

| 1485 kJ | 355 kcal | energy |
|---|---|---|
| | 19 g | protein |
| | 26 g | carbohydrate |
| | 3 g | sugars |
| | 19 g | fat |
| | 4 g | saturates |
| | 2 g | fiber |
| | 275 mg | sodium |

AFFORDABILITY
1

# ZUCCHINI & MINT
## *Frittata*

AFFORDABILITY
**1**

2 teaspoons olive oil
1 onion, thinly sliced
2 zucchini, thinly sliced
6 eggs
2 tablespoons coarsely chopped mint
salt and pepper

Serves **4**
Prep time **10 minutes**
Cooking time **25-35 minutes**

**1** Heat the oil in a heavy, nonstick 9-inch skillet with a heatproof handle. Stir in the onion and cook over a low heat, stirring occasionally, for 10 minutes until softened, then stir in the zucchini and cook, stirring, for an additional 2 minutes.

**2** Beat the eggs and mint together in a large bowl and season with salt and pepper. Stir in the cooked vegetables, then pour the mixture into the skillet and quickly arrange the vegetables so that they are evenly dispersed. Cook over a low heat for 8-10 minutes or until all but the top of the frittata is set.

**3** Finish cooking under a preheated very hot broiler, about 4 inches from the heat, until set but not colored. Give the pan a shake to loosen the frittata or use a spatula, then transfer to a plate to cool. Cut into wedges and serve slightly warm or at room temperature.

## Healthy tip

EGGS ARE A RELATIVELY CHEAP SOURCE OF GOOD PROTEIN AND ARE HIGH IN IRON AND VITAMINS A AND D. EGG YOLKS DO, HOWEVER, HAVE A HIGH CHOLESTEROL CONTENT, SO YOU SHOULD TRY TO LIMIT THE NUMBER YOU EAT EACH WEEK.

### Nutrient analysis per serving

| 666 kJ | 160 kcal | energy |
|---|---|---|
| | 12 g | protein |
| | 5 g | carbohydrate |
| | 1 g | sugars |
| | 11 g | fat |
| | 3 g | saturates |
| | 0 g | fiber |
| | 117 mg | sodium |

# MEXICAN-STYLE
## *Scrambled* EGGS

**1** Heat the oil in a large, heavy skillet and gently sauté the onion until soft. Pour in the beaten eggs, chopped tomatoes, and chiles. Season with salt.

**2** Gently stir the egg mixture over the heat until set to your taste. Transfer to a warm dish and serve immediately.

1½ tablespoons vegetable oil
½ onion, finely chopped
8 large eggs, beaten
3 plum tomatoes, skinned, seeded, and finely chopped
2 green chiles, chopped (seeded for a milder taste)
salt

Serves **4**
Prep time **10 minutes**
Cooking time **5-10 minutes**

## Good egg

This tried-and-tested formula means your "soldiers" won't be left languishing next to an overcooked egg. Put a few drops of vinegar into a pan of boiling water and carefully lower in your egg. Boil for 1 minute, then turn off the heat, cover the pan, and leave the egg for 6 minutes more. Remove and enjoy a perfectly cooked white and runny yolk.

### Nutrient analysis per serving

| | | |
|---|---|---|
| 900 kJ | 217 kcal | energy |
| | 15 g | protein |
| | 3 g | carbohydrate |
| | 3 g | sugars |
| | 16 g | fat |
| | 4 g | saturates |
| | 1 g | fiber |
| | 164 mg | sodium |

# ROASTED TOFU
## WITH *Szechuan Relish*

1½ tablespoons olive oil
14 oz silken firm tofu, cut into
   1-inch cubes

**Szechuan relish**
1¼ cups diced tomatoes (8 oz)
⅔ cup diced cucumber (3½ oz)
1 red chile, seeded and sliced
2 tablespoons thinly sliced green
   onions
½ garlic clove, crushed
½ teaspoon soft brown sugar
1 tablespoon lime juice
2 tablespoons chopped cilantro
½ teaspoon black pepper

Serves **4**
Prep time **10 minutes**
Cooking time **15-20 minutes**

**1** Pour the olive oil into a large, foil-lined roasting pan and spread it with a brush. Arrange the tofu cubes evenly over the oil. Put the roasting pan on the top shelf of a preheated oven, 475°F, and cook for 15-20 minutes or until the tofu is crisp and golden brown.

**2** Meanwhile, make the Szechuan relish. Combine all the ingredients in a bowl and mix well. Set aside.

**3** Put the roasted tofu cubes on a serving dish, spoon over the relish, and serve.

AFFORDABILITY **1**

### Nutrient analysis per serving

| 536 kJ | 129 kcal | energy |
|---|---|---|
| | 9 g | protein |
| | 3.9 g | carbohydrate |
| | 3.4 g | sugars |
| | 8.7 g | fat |
| | 1.2 g | saturates |
| | 0.9 g | fiber |
| | 12 mg | sodium |

AFFORDABILITY

**Nutrient analysis per serving**

| 166 kJ 39 kcal | energy |
|---|---|
| 1 g | protein |
| 7 g | carbohydrate |
| 1 g | sugars |
| 1 g | fat |
| 0 g | saturates |
| 1 g | fiber |
| 0.1 g | sodium |

# EGGPLANT &
# **POTATO** CAKES

1 Steam the eggplants and garlic for 6–8 minutes. Remove the garlic and peel, then mash them with the eggplants.

2 Steam the potatoes until cooked yet firm. Allow to cool, then grate coarsely and mix with the eggplants, onion, cilantro, salt, cumin, and paprika. Beat the egg white, fold it into the eggplant and potato mixture and leave for 5 minutes. Alternatively, to make shaping the cakes easier, put the mixture in the refrigerator for 5-10 minutes.

3 Oil your hands, take a portion of the mixture and form it into a 1¼-inch round. Heat the oil in a skillet and fry the cakes until golden all over. Alternatively, broil for 3–5 minutes on each side until lightly browned, although they won't be as crisp. Drain on double paper towels and eat hot or at room temperature.

1 lb eggplants, thickly sliced
4 garlic cloves, unpeeled
14 oz potatoes, scrubbed and left whole
2/3 cup grated onion (3½ oz)
¼ cup finely chopped cilantro leaves
¾ teaspoon salt
½ teaspoon ground cumin, or to taste
pinch of paprika
1 egg white
peanut oil, for oiling and frying

Serves **4**
Prep time **15 minutes, plus standing**
Cooking time **25-35 minutes**

# THREE **PEPPER** SALAD

2½ medium green bell peppers (8 oz)
2½ medium red bell peppers (8 oz)
2½ medium yellow bell peppers (8 oz)
1 small garlic clove
½ teaspoon salt
1 teaspoon apple cider vinegar
1¼ tablespoons lemon juice
1¼–1½ tablespoons extra virgin olive oil
¼ teaspoon ground cumin, or to taste
handful of parsley or cilantro leaves, finely chopped
pinch of black pepper (optional)

Serves **4**
Prep time **15 minutes**

1 Place the peppers on a heat diffuser (a metal circle that helps prevent pans from boiling over) or on a baking sheet over a medium gas flame and turn them for 3–5 minutes to char all over. Alternatively, preheat the broiler to high, broil the peppers for 18 minutes or until charred on all sides. Allow to cool, then skin, core, and seed. Slice the flesh into thin strips.

2 Meanwhile, use a mortar and pestle to mash the garlic and salt. Incorporate the vinegar, lemon juice, and oil and add to the peppers. Sprinkle with the cumin, parsley or cilantro and pepper, if used. Toss, taste, and adjust the seasonings if necessary, then serve.

**Nutrient analysis per serving**

| 420 kJ | 100 kcal | energy |
|---|---|---|
| | 3 g | protein |
| | 8 g | carbohydrate |
| | 8 g | sugars |
| | 6 g | fat |
| | 1 g | saturates |
| | 3 g | fiber |
| | 0.3 g | sodium |

# NAVY
## BEAN SALAD

1 Thoroughly rinse and drain the beans and put them in a large saucepan with a scant 2 cups water. Bring slowly to a boil, skimming the surface as foam forms, then reduce the heat to low, cover, and simmer for 20 minutes.

2 Add the onion, ginger, tomatoes, and oil and simmer, covered, for 15 minutes until the beans are tender.

3 A few minutes before the end of the cooking time, mash the tomatoes against the side of the pan, then add the turmeric, vinegar, salt, and pepper. Remove the pan from the heat, cover and leave until it reaches room temperature, then remove the ginger. Garnish with parsley sprigs, if desired, and serve.

1 cup dried navy beans, soaked for 6 hours
⅓ cup grated onions (2½ oz)
piece of fresh ginger root
4 oz tomatoes, skinned, seeded, and sliced into chunks (½ cup)
½ tablespoon extra virgin olive oil
½ teaspoon turmeric
2 teaspoons apple cider vinegar
½ teaspoon salt
pinch of black pepper
flat leaf parsley sprigs, to garnish (optional)

Serves **2-4**
Prep time **20 minutes, plus soaking**
Cooking time **35 minutes**

### Nutrient analysis per serving

| | | |
|---|---|---|
| 1436 kJ | 338 kcal | energy |
| | 23 g | protein |
| | 57 g | carbohydrate |
| | 9 g | sugars |
| | 4 g | fat |
| | 1 g | saturates |
| | 25 g | fiber |
| | 0.8 g | sodium |

# BACHELOR OF BUDGET
## BAKES & PUDS

VICTORIA SPONGE CAKE

SCONES WITH WHIPPED CREAM

# CHOCOLATE CHIP
# COOKIES

¼ lb (1 stick) unsalted butter, softened, plus extra for greasing
¼ cup light brown sugar
1 egg, beaten
1¼ cups self-rising flour
4 oz semisweet chocolate, finely chopped

Makes **25**
Prep time **10 minutes**
Cooking time **15-20 minutes**

1 Use the extra butter to lightly grease a cookie sheet to prevent the cookies from sticking.

2 Put the butter and sugar in a mixing bowl and beat together with a wooden spoon until light and fluffy. Beat in the egg, then sift in the flour. Add the chocolate pieces and mix thoroughly.

3 Put 25 teaspoonfuls of the mixture slightly apart on the cookie sheet and bake in a preheated oven, 350°F, for 15-20 minutes until golden brown.

4 Leave on the cookie sheet for 1 minute, then transfer to a cooling rack and allow to cool.

# PEANUT BUTTER COOKIES

**1** Use the extra butter to lightly grease three large cookie sheets to prevent the cookies from sticking.

**2** Beat the butter and sugar together in a mixing bowl or a food processor until pale and creamy. Add the peanut butter, egg, flour, and baking powder and stir together until combined. Stir in the peanuts.

**3** Drop large teaspoonfuls of the mixture onto the cookie sheets, leaving 2-inch gaps between each for them to spread during cooking. Flatten the mounds slightly and bake in a preheated oven, 375°F, for 12 minutes until golden around the edges.

**4** Allow to cool on the cookie sheets for 2 minutes then transfer to a cooling rack to cool completely.

¼ lb (1 stick) unsalted butter, at room temperature, plus extra for greasing
¾ cup brown sugar
½ cup chunky peanut butter
1 egg, lightly beaten
1¼ cups all-purpose flour
½ teaspoon baking powder
½ cup unsalted peanuts

Makes **32**
Prep time **10 minutes**
Cooking time **12 minutes**

AFFORDABILITY

# FROSTED **CHOCOLATE** WHOOPIES

unsalted butter, for greasing
1¼ cups self-rising flour
¼ teaspoon baking soda
¼ cup unsweetened cocoa
  powder
½ cup unrefined superfine sugar
2 tablespoons vanilla sugar
1 egg
3 tablespoons vegetable oil
1 tablespoon milk
2 oz semisweet or milk
  chocolate, chopped

**Filling**
½ cup cream cheese
2 tablespoons confectioners'
  sugar, sifted
1 teaspoon finely grated orange
  zest
few drops of orange extract
  (optional)

Makes **12-14**
Prep time **20 minutes, plus
cooling**
Cooking time **15 minutes**

1 Use the butter to lightly grease a large cookie sheet to prevent the whoopies from sticking.

2 Put the flour, baking soda, cocoa powder, and sugars in a bowl. Beat the egg with the vegetable oil and milk and add to the dry ingredients. Beat together to form a thick paste, adding a little more milk if the mixture feels crumbly.

3 Take teaspoonfuls of the mixture, flour your hands and roll the mixture into balls, about the size of a cherry. Space well apart on the cookie sheet and flatten slightly.

4 Bake in a preheated oven, 400°F, for 12 minutes until the mixture has spread and is pale golden. Transfer to a cooling rack to cool.

5 Beat together the cream cheese, confectioners' sugar, orange zest, and extract and use it to sandwich the cakes together.

6 Put the chocolate in a small heatproof bowl over a pan of simmering water, making sure that the bottom of the bowl does not sit in the water. Melt the chocolate and spread it over the tops of the whoopies. (Alternatively, melt the chocolate in the microwave in 10-20 second bursts.)

AFFORDABILITY
2

# CHOCOLATE MOCHA BROWNIES

AFFORDABILITY
2

*LIKE ALL THE BEST BROWNIE RECIPES, THIS VERSION IS BOTH GOOEY AND FUDGY.*

1 Grease and line a shallow 11 x 7 inch rectangular pan or a 9-inch square pan.

2 Melt the semisweet chocolate with the butter in a heatproof bowl over a pan of simmering water, stirring frequently, until smooth. Stir in the coffee.

3 In a separate bowl beat together the eggs and sugar. Stir in the melted chocolate mixture, sift the flour and baking powder into the bowl, and stir until they are combined.

4 Add the chopped milk chocolate and turn the mixture into the pan. Level the surface and bake in a preheated oven, 375°F, for about 30 minutes or until a crust has formed but the mixture feels quite soft underneath. Allow to cool in the pan, then cut into squares.

¼ lb plus 4 tablespoons (1½ sticks) unsalted butter, plus extra for greasing
8 oz semisweet chocolate, broken up
2 tablespoons instant coffee
3 eggs
generous 1 cup light brown sugar
generous ½ cup self-rising flour
½ teaspoon baking powder
7 oz milk chocolate, coarsely chopped

Makes **15**
Prep time **15 minutes**
Cooking time **30 minutes**

## Freshen up your refrigerator

It doesn't take much more than a leftover take-out or a piece of ripe cheese to make your refrigerator smell like it should be condemned. Obviously, you need to remove the culinary culprits to stop the odors escalating, but a slice or two from a fresh lemon will help to freshen things up.

# JIM JAMS

¼ lb (1 stick) unsalted butter
⅔ cup light corn syrup
generous ½ cup light brown sugar
1 cup oats
1 cup self-rising whole-wheat flour
¼ cup shredded, dried coconut

**To finish**
3 tablespoons strawberry jelly
2 tablespoons shredded, dried
   coconut

Makes **9**
Prep time **10 minutes**
Cooking time **15-20 minutes**

1 Line an 7-inch shallow square cake pan with nonstick
   parchment paper.

2 Melt butter, syrup, and sugar gently in a saucepan. Remove
   from the heat to stir in the oats, flour, and coconut.

3 Press into an even layer in the pan and bake in a preheated
   oven, 350°F, for 15 minutes until golden.

4 Allow to cool in the pan for 10 minutes, then mark into nine
   squares. Spread with the jelly and sprinkle with the
coconut. Allow to cool completely.

5 Lift the paper out of the pan, cut the squares right
   through, and peel off the paper. Store in an airtight
container for up to three days.

AFFORDABILITY
2

# SCONES WITH *Whipped Cream*

**1** Sift the flour, cream of tartar, baking soda, and salt into a mixing bowl and blend in the butter with your fingertips until the mixture resembles bread crumbs. Stir in the sugar and add enough milk to mix to a soft dough.

**2** Turn onto a floured surface, knead lightly, and roll out to ¾ inch thick. Cut into 2-inch rounds with a cookie cutter. Place on a floured cookie sheet and brush with milk.

**3** Bake in a preheated oven, 425°F, for 10 minutes and transfer to a cooling rack to cool. Serve with butter and preserves or with whipped cream and preserves.

2 cups all-purpose flour
1 teaspoon cream of tartar
½ teaspoon baking soda
pinch of salt
4 tablespoons unsalted butter, chilled and diced
2 tablespoons superfine sugar
about ½ cup milk, plus extra to glaze

**To serve**
butter or whipped cream
strawberry preserves

Makes **10**
Prep time **10 minutes**
Cooking time **10 minutes**

AFFORDABILITY
**1**

# ROCK BUNS

AFFORDABILITY
2

THESE ARE QUICK AND EASY TO WHIZ UP AND LOVELY WHEN EATEN FRESHLY BAKED. DON'T LET THEM HANG AROUND FOR TOO LONG THOUGH, OR THEY WILL LIVE UP TO THEIR INAPPROPRIATE NAME.

¼ lb (1 stick) unsalted butter, softened, plus extra for greasing
½ cup unrefined superfine sugar
1¾ cups self-rising flour
1 teaspoon ground ginger
1 teaspoon ground cinnamon
1 egg, beaten
⅔ cup milk
½ cup golden raisins
½ cup currants
15 white sugar cubes, about 2 oz

Makes **20**
Prep time **10 minutes**
Cooking time **15 minutes**

1 Use the extra butter to lightly grease two cookie sheets to prevent the buns from sticking.

2 Cream together the butter and sugar until light and fluffy. Stir in the flour, spices, egg, and milk and mix to a soft dough. Stir the dried fruits into the mixture.

3 Place dessertspoonfuls of the mixture on the cookie sheets, spacing them slightly apart.

4 Put the sugar cubes in a plastic bag and lightly crush with a rolling pin. Sprinkle over the buns and bake in a preheated oven, 375°F, for about 15 minutes or until risen and golden. Transfer to a cooling rack to cool.

# BANANA **MUFFINS**

1  Line a deep muffin pan with 10 muffin cups or lightly grease the cups.

2  Sift the flour, baking powder, and cinnamon into a bowl. Stir in the nutmeg, almonds, and sugar.

3  Lightly mash the bananas and mix in the eggs, oil, milk, and honey to make a sloppy paste. Work the banana mixture into the dry ingredients, first using a fork and then folding in with a tablespoon.

4  Spoon the muffin batter into the paper cups or greased sections and bake in a preheated oven, 375°F, for 25 minutes (check after 20 minutes) or until well risen. When they are done a toothpick inserted in the center should come out clean. Leave for 5 minutes, then transfer to a cooling rack to cool.

scant 1²⁄₃ cups all-purpose flour
1 tablespoon baking powder
1½ teaspoons ground cinnamon
grated nutmeg
½ cup ground almonds
¼ cup brown sugar
2 large ripe bananas, about 11½ oz
  unpeeled or 8 oz peeled
2 eggs
2 tablespoons sunflower oil
½ cup fat-free milk
3 tablespoons honey

Makes **10**
Prep time **20 minutes**
Cooking time **20-25 minutes**

## Keep your oven clean

Ovens are a serious pain to clean, so anything you can do to avoid this loathsome task is a benefit. Line broiler pans and oven pans with a layer of kitchen foil, tucking it down so that the sides of the pans are protected too. When they get really dirty, you can swap the foil and the pans will be pristine.

AFFORDABILITY
2

# BLUEBERRY & VANILLA MUFFINS

AFFORDABILITY
2

1⅓ cups ground almonds
¾ cup unrefined superfine sugar
⅓ cup self-rising flour
¼ lb plus 4 tablespoons (1½
    sticks) unsalted butter, melted
4 egg whites
1 teaspoon vanilla extract
1¼ cups blueberries

Makes **10**
Prep time **5 minutes**
Cooking time **15 minutes**

**1** Line 10 sections of a muffin pan with paper muffin cups or grease the sections.

**2** Mix together the ground almonds, sugar, flour, and butter. Add the egg whites and vanilla extract and combine until the mixture is a smooth paste.

**3** Spoon into the cups and sprinkle with the blueberries. Bake in a preheated oven, 425°F, for 15 minutes until just firm in the center. Leave for 5 minutes, then transfer the muffins to a cooling rack to cool.

# TRIPLE
## CHOCOLATE
# MUFFINS

⅓ cup semisweet chocolate chips
4 tablespoons unsalted butter
2 eggs
⅓ cup superfine sugar
generous ½ cup self-rising flour
¼ cup unsweetened cocoa powder
2 tablespoons white chocolate
  chips

Makes **10**
Prep time **12 minutes**
Cooking time **12 minutes**

1 Line 10 sections of a muffin pan with paper cups or grease the sections.

2 Carefully melt the semisweet chocolate chips with the butter in a small, heavy pan set over a low heat.

3 Beat together the eggs, sugar, flour, and cocoa powder in a large bowl. With a metal spatula, fold in the melted chocolate mixture and the white chocolate chips.

4 Spoon the mixture into the paper cups and bake in a preheated oven, 350°F, for 12 minutes or until risen and firm to the touch. Transfer the muffins to a cooling rack to cool slightly before eating.

# VICTORIA SPONGE CAKE

**1** Use the extra butter to lightly grease two 7-inch layer pans and line the bases with a circle of waxed paper or nonstick parchment paper.

**2** Put the butter and sugar in a mixing bowl and beat together with a wooden spoon until pale and creamy. Gradually beat in the eggs and vanilla extract, a little at a time, adding 1 tablespoon of flour with each addition to help prevent the mixture from curdling.

**3** Sift the remaining flour and baking powder into the bowl and fold gently into the creamed mixture.

**4** Spoon the batter into the cake pans and spread the tops level. Bake in a preheated oven, 350°F, for about 20 minutes or until the cake will spring back when lightly pressed with a fingertip. Allow to cool for 5 minutes, then loosen and turn the cakes out onto a cooling rack, peel off the lining paper, and allow to cool.

**5** Put one of the cakes, top downward, on a serving plate and spread with the jelly. Top with the second cake and dust the top with sifted confectioners' sugar.

¼ lb plus 4 tablespoons (1½ sticks) unsalted butter, at room temperature, plus extra for greasing
generous ¾ cup superfine sugar
3 eggs
1 teaspoon vanilla extract
scant 1½ cups self-rising flour
1 teaspoon baking powder
3 tablespoons strawberry jelly
confectioners' sugar, for dusting

Serves **8**
Prep time **15 minutes**
Cooking time **20-25 minutes**

# LEMON
## *Drizzle*
# CAKE

ASK ANYONE TO LIST THEIR FAVORITE CAKES, AND THIS WILL ALMOST CERTAINLY BE ONE OF THEM.

½ lb (2 sticks) unsalted butter, softened, plus extra for greasing
generous 1 cup superfine sugar
finely grated zest of 3 lemons
4 eggs, beaten
2 cups self-rising flour
1 teaspoon baking powder
¾ cup ground almonds
scant ½ cup lemon juice
½ cup granulated sugar

Serves **8-10**
Prep time **20 minutes**
Cooking time **50-60 minutes**

1 Grease and line the base and sides of an 8-inch round cake pan or an 7-inch square pan. Lightly grease the paper.

2 Cream together the butter, superfine sugar, and lemon zest until light and fluffy. Beat in the eggs, a little at a time, beating well between each addition. Add a little of the flour if the mixture starts to curdle.

3 Sift the flour and baking powder into the bowl, add the ground almonds and 2 tablespoons lemon juice, and gently fold in using a large metal spoon.

4 Turn the mixture into the pan and level the surface. Bake in a preheated oven, 350°F, for about 45 minutes or until just firm and a toothpick inserted into the center comes out clean.

5 Meanwhile, mix together the remaining lemon juice with the granulated sugar. Transfer the cake to a cooling rack. Give the lemon mixture a good stir and spoon it over the cake. As the cake cools the syrup will sink into the cake, leaving a sugary crust.

# CARROT
# CAKE

1 Lightly grease and line the base and sides of an 8-inch round cake pan.

2 Put the butter, sugar, eggs, orange zest, flour, baking powder, ground nuts, and ginger together in a bowl and beat until smooth and creamy.

3 Stir in the carrots and raisins until evenly combined and turn the batter into the pan. Level the surface and bake in a preheated oven, 350°F, for about 1 hour or until just firm and a toothpick inserted into the center comes out clean. Transfer to a cooling rack to cool.

4 Make the cream cheese frosting. Put the cream cheese in a bowl and beat until it is softened and smooth. Add 1 teaspoon lemon juice and the confectioners' sugar and beat until smooth, adding a little more juice if the mixture is too firm.

5 Use a spatula to spread the top and sides of the cake with the frosting. Decorate with toasted hazelnuts.

½ lb (2 sticks) unsalted butter, softened, plus extra for greasing
generous 1 cup light brown sugar
4 eggs
grated zest of 1 orange
scant 1½ cups self-rising flour, sifted
1 teaspoon baking powder, sifted
¾ cup ground hazelnuts
3 preserved stem gingers, chopped
1⅔ cups finely shredded carrots (10 oz)
½ cup raisins
toasted hazelnuts, coarsely chopped, to decorate

**Cream cheese frosting**
scant 1 cup full-fat cream cheese
1-2 teaspoons lime or lemon juice
½ cup confectioners' sugar, sifted

Serves **10-12**
Prep time **30 minutes**
Cooking time **1 hour**

# CHOCOLATE FUDGE CUPCAKES

scant ½ cup unsweetened cocoa powder
scant ½ cup boiling water
4 tablespoons lightly salted butter, softened
generous ½ cup light brown sugar
1 egg
¾ cup self-rising flour
1¼ cups raspberries, to decorate

**Frosting**
3 oz semisweet chocolate, chopped
1 tablespoon milk
2 tablespoons lightly salted butter
2 heaping tablespoons confectioners' sugar, plus extra for dusting

Makes **16**
Prep time **25 minutes, plus cooling**
Cooking time **12 minutes**

1 Put 16 mini silicone heatproof muffin cups onto a cookie sheet.

2 Beat the cocoa powder with the boiling water in a bowl. Allow to cool.

3 Beat together the butter and brown sugar in a separate bowl until pale and creamy. Gradually beat in the egg. Sift in the flour and stir in the cocoa mixture.

4 Spoon the batter into the cups and bake in a preheated oven, 350°F, for 8-10 minutes until risen and just firm. Leave in the cups for 2 minutes, then transfer to a cooling rack.

5 Put the chocolate, milk, and butter in a saucepan and heat gently until melted and a smooth sauce forms. Remove from the heat. Sift the confectioners' sugar into the chocolate mixture and stir well. Use a spatula to spread the frosting over the cakes. Allow to cool completely. Sprinkle with the raspberries and serve lightly dusted with confectioners' sugar.

AFFORDABILITY 1

# MALTY FRUIT CAKE

THIS IS AN EASY AND WHOLESOME CAKE, PERFECT FOR WHEN YOU WANT TO MAKE SOMETHING QUICKLY FOR TEA OR SNACKS.

**1** Grease and line the base and sides of a 6-cup loaf pan, making the paper come at least ½ inch above the rim of the pan. Grease the paper.

**2** Mix together the fruit, sugar, malt extract, bran, spices, and milk in a bowl and allow to stand for 20 minutes.

**3** Stir in the flour, turn the mixture into the pan, and bake in a preheated oven, 325°F, for about 50 minutes or until a toothpick inserted into the center comes out clean. Transfer to a cooling rack to cool.

unsalted butter, for greasing
1 cup luxury mixed dried fruit
generous ½ cup dark brown sugar
3 tablespoons malt extract
1½ cups shredded bran or bran-flake cereal
1 teaspoon ground cinnamon
½ teaspoon grated nutmeg
1¼ cups milk
1¼ cups self-rising flour

Serves **8**
Prep time **10 minutes, plus soaking**
Cooking time **50 minutes**

# SWEET
# CHEATS

◇◇◇◇◇◇◇◇◇◇◇◇◇◇◇◇◇◇◇◇◇◇◇◇◇◇◇◇◇◇◇◇◇◇◇◇◇◇◇◇◇◇◇◇◇

There's nothing like a lovingly prepared dessert for a show-stopping dinner party finale, but if you've been sweating over a hot stove all day long just to get a main course on the table, you might have left yourself a bit short of time to rustle up a dessert. If so, don't panic – help is at hand. With a few basic ingredients you can create a happy ending for your meal that will wow your mates but won't send you over the culinary edge.

## ICE CREAM SURPRISE

Ice cream might sound like a cop-out for dessert, but not if you jazz it up with a few surprises. Buy a carton of any ordinary, plain vanilla ice cream and a selection of small candies. Let the ice cream soften slightly for a minute or two, then mix in the candies and pop the ice cream back in the freezer. If you have a sudden last-minute burst of creativity, you could serve it with Glossy Chocolate Sauce (see page 236) spooned over the top.

## HOT CHOCOLAT

Not strictly speaking a des
but hot chocolate with cr
and mini marshmallo
always a

## FEELING FRUITY

This does, it must be said, involve a tiny bit of cooking, but it's nothing more complicated than turning on the oven—honestly. Turn on the oven to about 400°F, and, while you're waiting for it to reach the required temperature, cut in half as many peaches as you have guests and take out the pits. Put the peaches on a baking sheet and drizzle over a little orange juice, fruit liqueur, or red wine, then sprinkle generously with brown sugar. Bake the peaches for about 20 minutes and serve with a dollop of ice cream or cream.

## ETON MESS

This dessert is so easy to make. Break up some mini store-bought meringue nests into a large mixing bowl (try to get a mixture of chunky and fine pieces), add some chopped strawberries and raspberries and a carton of extra thick cream. Mix carefully so that the berries don't completely disintegrate, then spoon the mixture into your best serving dishes and serve.

## TRICK TRIFLE

Who doesn't like sponge cake, fruit, and custard piled high into a bowl? Select your biggest glasses and line the bases with pieces of store-bought sponge cake. Put pieces of chopped canned fruit into the glasses, spooning a bit of the juice over as well. Then pour over some prepared custard and sprinkle with chocolate shavings or sprinkles. Put the trifles in the refrigerator until you're ready to eat them.

# PANCAKE STACK
## WITH **MAPLE SYRUP**

1 egg
generous ½ cup all-purpose flour,
   sifted
scant ½ cup milk
2½ tablespoons vegetable oil
1 tablespoon superfine sugar
maple syrup, for drizzling
8 scoops of vanilla ice cream, to
   serve

Serves **4**
Prep time **10 minutes**
Cooking time **6 minutes**

**1** Make the batter. Put the egg, flour, milk, oil, and sugar in a blender or food processor and whiz until smooth and creamy.

**2** Heat a skillet over a medium heat and pour a ladleful of the batter into each corner to make four pancakes. After about 1 minute the tops of the pancakes will start to set and air bubbles will rise to the top and burst. Use a spatula to turn the pancakes over and cook on the other side for 1 minute.

**3** Repeat twice more until you have used all the batter, making 12 small pancakes in all. Bring to the table as a stack, drizzled with maple syrup. Serve three pancakes to each person with two scoops of ice cream.

# VANILLA *&* BANANA
# PANCAKES

AFFORDABILITY 1

**1** Mash the bananas with the vanilla extract in a bowl to make a smooth puree. Sift the flour and baking powder into a separate bowl and stir in the sugar.

**2** Beat the egg, milk, and melted butter together in another bowl and beat into the dry ingredients until smooth. Stir in the banana puree.

**3** Heat a little oil in a large skillet or griddle pan over a medium heat. Using a large metal spoon, drop four spoonfuls of the batter, well spaced apart, in the pan and cook for 2 minutes or until bubbles form on the surfaces and the undersides are golden brown. Use a spatula to turn the pancakes over and cook on the other side for 1–2 minutes. Remove from the pan, wrap in a dish towel, and keep warm while you cook the remaining batter in the same way.

**4** Transfer the pancakes to a serving plate and serve with maple syrup.

2 ripe bananas
1 teaspoon vanilla extract
1¼ cups self-rising flour
1 teaspoon baking powder
1 tablespoon superfine sugar
1 egg
⅓ cup milk
1 tablespoon unsalted butter, melted
sunflower oil, for frying
maple syrup, to serve

Serves **4**
Prep time **15 minutes**
Cooking time **15 minutes**

# BUTTERMILK **PANCAKES** WITH **BLUEBERRY** SAUCE

2 cups fresh blueberries
2 tablespoons honey
dash of lemon juice
1 tablespoon unsalted butter
1¼ cups self-rising flour
1 teaspoon baking soda
3 tablespoons superfine sugar
1 egg, beaten
1½ cups buttermilk, Greek-style
   yogurt or sour cream, to serve
confectioners' sugar, for dusting

Serves **4-6**
Prep time **10 minutes**
Cooking time **16 minutes**

1 Put the berries, honey, and a dash of lemon juice in a small saucepan and warm gently for about 3 minutes until the berries release their juices. Keep warm.

2 Melt the butter in a small pan. Sift the flour and baking soda together into a bowl and stir in the sugar. Beat the egg and buttermilk together and gradually beat into the dry ingredients with the melted butter to make a smooth batter.

3 Heat a nonstick skillet until hot and drop in large spoonfuls of batter. Cook for 3 minutes, until bubbles appear on the surface. Use a spatula to turn the pancakes over and cook for another minute. Keep warm while you cook the remainder.

4 Serve the pancakes topped with the blueberry sauce and some Greek-style yogurt or sour cream. Dust with confectioners' sugar before serving.

AFFORDABILITY
2

# Toffee Apple
# BAKE

1 Toss the apples in a shallow heatproof dish with 1 tablespoonful of the flour and the brown sugar.

2 Mix the remaining flour with the superfine sugar and spice in a bowl. Add the egg, yogurt, and butter and stir lightly until only just combined.

3 Spoon the mixture over the apples and bake in a preheated oven, 425°F, for 15-20 minutes until just firm and golden. Serve warm.

3 dessert apples, cored and thickly sliced
¾ cup self-rising flour, plus 1 tablespoon extra
generous ½ cup light brown sugar
¼ cup superfine sugar
½ teaspoon ground allspice
1 egg
scant ½ cup plain yogurt
4 tablespoons unsalted butter, melted

Serves **4**
Prep time **10 minutes**
Cooking time **15-20 minutes**

## Milking it

Fact: student houses always run out of milk. Fact: you can freeze milk. So if you don't want to develop the taste for black tea and coffee, keep a sneaky carton of milk tucked away at the back of the freezer, and you won't have to choose between curdled milk or an early-morning trip to the store.

# *Sticky* TOFFEE PUDDINGS

¼ cup whipping cream, plus extra to serve
4 tablespoons butter, separated into quarters
¼ cup light brown sugar

**Pudding**
¼ cup walnuts, finely chopped
¼ lb (1 stick) unsalted butter, softened
generous ½ cup soft light brown sugar
2 eggs
generous ½ cup self-rising flour

Serves **4**
Prep time **5 minutes**
Cooking time **20-25 minutes**

**1** Divide the cream, butter, and sugar evenly into four ramekins or timbales.

**2** Make the pudding. Put the walnuts, butter, sugar, eggs, and flour in a food processor and process until smooth. Spoon the batter over the toffee mixture and smooth flat.

**3** Bake in a preheated oven, 375°F, for 20-25 minutes until risen and lightly golden. Turn out and serve with extra cream, lightly whipped.

AFFORDABILITY 2

# CHOCOLATE
## BREAD & BUTTER
### *Pudding*

**1** Lightly grease a 5-cup shallow, round, heatproof pie dish.

**2** Slice the croissants thickly and spread the butter over one side of each cut face. Stand the croissant slices upright and close together in the dish to completely fill it.

**3** Mix together the sugar and spice and spoon over the croissants and between the gaps. Stand the dish in a large roasting pan.

**4** Beat together the milk, eggs, and vanilla extract and strain into the dish. Allow to stand for 15 minutes.

**5** Pour hot water into the roasting pan to come halfway up the sides of the pie dish and bake in a preheated oven, 350°F, for about 25 minutes until the pudding is golden and the custard just set.

**6** Lift the dish out of the roasting pan, dust with sifted confectioners' sugar and serve the pudding warm with a little pouring cream.

4 tablespoons unsalted butter, plus extra for greasing
4 chocolate croissants
¼ cup superfine sugar
¼ teaspoon ground allspice
1¼ cups milk
4 eggs
1 teaspoon vanilla extract
confectioners' sugar, for dusting
pouring cream, to serve

Serves **4**
Prep time **20 minutes, plus standing**
Cooking time **25 minutes**

# LEMON
## *Puddle*
# PUDDING

6 tablespoons unsalted butter, at room temperature, plus extra for greasing
¾ cup superfine sugar
grated zest of 2 lemons
3 eggs, separated
generous ⅓ cup self-rising flour, sifted
1¼ cups milk
¼ cup lemon juice
confectioners' sugar, for dusting (optional)

Serves **4**
Prep time **20 minutes**
Cooking time **25-30 minutes**

1 Lightly grease a 5-cup pie dish and stand the dish in a roasting pan.

2 Put the butter in a mixing bowl with the sugar and lemon zest. Beat the egg whites in a separate bowl until they are softly peaking. Using the still dirty whisk, beat the butter, sugar, and lemon zest until light and fluffy, then mix in the flour and egg yolks.

3 Combine the milk and lemon juice gradually until only just mixed. (The mixture may appear to separate slightly but this will disappear during baking.) Add to the batter.

4 Fold in the egg whites, then gently pour the mixture into the pie dish. Pour hot water into the roasting pan to come halfway up the sides of the dish and bake in a preheated oven, 375°F, for about 25 minutes until slightly risen, golden brown, and the top has begun to crack. Insert a knife into the center: the top two-thirds should be soufflé-like and the bottom third a saucy, custard-like layer. If it's very soft in the center, cook for an extra 5 minutes.

5 Dust the top with a little sifted confectioners' sugar, if desired, then serve immediately spooned into shallow bowls. Don't allow the dessert to stand or the topping will absorb the sauce.

# BAKED
## PEAR
### WITH ALMOND
## CRUMBLE

generous ½ cup whole-wheat
  flour
generous ½ cup ground almonds
⅓ cup light brown sugar
5 tablespoons unsalted butter,
  diced
4 pears, quartered, cored, and
  sliced lengthwise
juice of 1 lime
2 tablespoons sliced almonds
⅔ cup sour cream, to serve
  (optional)

Serves **4**
Prep time **10 minutes**
Cooking time **20 minutes**

**1** Mix together the flour, ground almonds, and sugar in a
large bowl. Add the butter and blend in with your
fingertips until the mixture resembles fine bread crumbs.

**2** Arrange the pear slices in four deep heatproof
ramekins and drizzle with the lime juice. Cover the
pears with the crumble mixture and sprinkle with the sliced
almonds.

**3** Bake in a preheated oven, 425°F, for 20 minutes.
Serve warm, topped with sour cream, if desired.

# RICE Pudding

AFFORDABILITY **1**

1 Rinse the rice briefly under cold water to remove any impurities, drain, and soak for 15 minutes in boiling water. Rinse well and drain.

2 Put the milk, sugar, salt, vanilla bean, cinnamon stick, and lime and orange zest in a heavy saucepan and bring slowly to a boil, stirring constantly. Remove from the heat and allow to infuse for 10 minutes. Remove the lime and orange zest and discard. Remove the vanilla bean, slit it open, and scrape out the seeds into the milk.

3 Add the rice to the milk and bring to a boil over a medium heat. Reduce the heat, cover, and gently simmer until the rice is cooked and the mixture thickens. Stir in the raisins. You may need some more cold milk to adjust the consistency: the rice must not be dry.

4 Remove from the heat and allow to cool, then transfer the pudding to a serving dish, cover, and refrigerate until required. Serve cold, dusted with cinnamon to decorate.

1 cup short grain white rice
6¼ cups low-fat milk
½ cup superfine sugar
pinch of salt
1 vanilla bean
1 cinnamon stick, broken into 2-3 pieces
thinly pared zest of 1 lime
thinly pared zest of 1 orange
⅓ cup raisins
ground cinnamon, for dusting

Serves **6-8**
Prep time **10 minutes, plus soaking and infusing**
Cooking time **15 minutes**

# **CHOCOLATE** RISOTTO

2½ cups milk
2 tablespoons sugar
4 tablespoons butter
generous ½ cup arborio or
  carnaroli rice
⅓ cup hazelnuts, toasted and
  chopped
⅓ cup golden raisins
scant 1 cup grated good-quality
  semisweet chocolate
splash of brandy (optional)
grated chocolate, to decorate

Serves **4**
Prep time **5 minutes**
Cooking time **20 minutes**

1 Put the milk and sugar into a saucepan and heat to simmering point.

2 Melt the butter in a heavy saucepan, add the rice, and stir well to coat the grains.

3 Add a ladleful of hot milk to the rice and stir well. When the rice has absorbed the milk, add another ladleful. Continue to add the milk in stages and stir until it is all absorbed. The rice should be just tender with a creamy sauce.

4 Add the hazelnuts, golden raisins, and grated chocolate and mix quickly. Serve decorated with a little grated chocolate. Try not to overmix the chocolate because the marbled effect looks good. For a special treat, add a splash of brandy just before decorating and serving the risotto.

AFFORDABILITY

3

# CHOCOLATE *&*
# RASPBERRY
## *Pudding*

olive oil spray, for oiling
1¼ cups fresh raspberries
1 cup self-rising flour
scant ½ cup unsweetened cocoa
   powder
½ cup superfine sugar
1 cup milk
6 tablespoons unsalted butter,
   melted
2 eggs, beaten

**Topping**
⅓ cup superfine sugar
⅓ cup light brown sugar
2 tablespoons unsweetened cocoa
   powder
1½ cups boiling water
confectioners' sugar, for dusting

Serves **6**
Prep time **15 minutes, plus
resting**
Cooking time **40-45 minutes**

1 Spray a 4-cup baking dish lightly with spray olive oil to
prevent the pudding from sticking.

2 Sprinkle a layer of raspberries evenly over the base of
the dish.

3 Sift the flour and cocoa powder into a bowl and stir in the
superfine sugar. Make a well in the center and beat in the
milk, melted butter, and eggs to form a smooth batter (the
batter should be quite runny). Pour the mixture into the dish,
covering the raspberries.

4 Make the topping. Combine the sugars and cocoa powder
and sprinkle over the top of the chocolate mixture.
Carefully pour the boiling water over the top of the mixture as
evenly as possible.

5 Bake in a preheated oven, 350°F, for 40-45 minutes until
the pudding is firm to the touch and some "bubbles" of
sauce appear on the top. Rest for 5 minutes, then dust with
confectioners' sugar and serve.

# Sticky Rice WITH MANGO

1¼ cups white sticky rice
scant ½ cup coconut milk
2 tablespoons palm or coconut
   sugar
½ teaspoon salt (optional)
4 ripe mangoes

Serves **4**
Prep time **20 minutes, plus
soaking and resting**
Cooking time **30-35 minutes**

**1** Soak the rice in a bowl of water for at least 3 hours. Drain the rice and transfer it to a steamer basket lined with a double thickness of cheesecloth. Spread the rice in the steamer.

**2** Bring the water to a rolling boil. Taking care not to burn your hand, set the steamer basket over the water, reduce the heat, cover, and steam for 20-25 minutes or until the rice swells and is glistening and tender. Check and replenish the water every 10 minutes or so.

**3** Mix the coconut milk and sugar with 3 tablespoons water in a small saucepan and stir over a low heat until the sugar has dissolved.

**4** As soon as the rice is cooked, spoon it into a bowl, mix it with the coconut milk mixture, cover, and allow to rest for 10 minutes.

**5** Peel the mangoes and slice off the outside cheeks of each, removing as much flesh as you can in large pieces. (Avoid cutting very close to the pit where the flesh is fibrous.) Discard the pit. Slice each piece of mango into 4-5 pieces lengthwise, arrange on a serving plate, and spoon a portion of sticky rice and coconut milk next to them.

AFFORDABILITY
**1**

# CARAMELIZED ORANGE & PINEAPPLE

4 oranges
generous ¾ cup sugar
1 small pineapple

Serves **4**
Prep time **10 minutes**
Cooking time **10 minutes**

1 Use a small, sharp knife to remove the zest from two of the oranges and slice it into very fine strips. Put the zest in a saucepan of boiling water and simmer for 2 minutes. Remove and drain well.

2 Put the sugar in a heavy saucepan, add ½ cup water, and heat gently, swishing the pan constantly until the sugar is dissolved. Increase the heat and boil the syrup until it turns golden brown. Take care not to overcook the caramel; if it gets too dark, carefully add 2 tablespoons of water. Stand back when you add the water because the caramel will spit. Set aside when ready.

3 To peel the oranges, cut a slice off the top and bottom of each one, then place the orange on one of these cut sides and take a knife around the side of the orange, cutting away the skin and pith. Cut across the orange into about 6-7 slices.

4 To prepare the pineapple, top and tail it and slice away the skin from top to bottom. Make sure that you remove the "eyes" close to the skin. Cut the pineapple into quarters and remove the core. Cut into slices.

5 Make alternate layers of orange and pineapple in a heatproof dish. Sprinkle with the orange zest, pour over the caramel, and allow to stand until required.

AFFORDABILITY

1

# BAKED **PEACHES**
# WITH ALMONDS
# *&* HONEY

4 tablespoons unsalted butter,
   plus extra for greasing
4 large ripe peaches, halved and
   pitted
2/3 cup sliced almonds
¼ cup honey
a little ground cinnamon
sour cream, to serve

Serves **4**
Prep time **5 minutes**
Cooking time **15 minutes**

**1** Butter a shallow baking dish that is large enough to hold 8 peach halves.

**2** Put the peaches in the baking dish, skin side down, and dot with butter. Sprinkle with the almonds, drizzle with the honey, and dust with cinnamon.

**3** Bake the peaches at the top of a preheated oven, 400°F, for 10-15 minutes, until there is a little color in the peaches and the almonds have browned slightly.

**4** Serve the peaches with the juices drizzled over and topped with a spoonful of sour cream.

# PANETTONE
# **PUDDING**

**1** Use the butter to grease the bottom and sides of a 5-cup heatproof dish.

**2** Spread the panettone slices with apricot preserves and cut them into triangles or rectangles. Arrange them in the dish in overlapping layers.

**3** Put the milk and cream into a saucepan and bring gently to a boil.

**4** Beat together the eggs, egg yolk, and sugar in a bowl until creamy and fluffy. Continue beating and slowly add the hot milk and cream. When it is all combined, carefully pour it over the panettone slices, making sure they are completely covered by the custard mixture. Sprinkle with a little extra sugar to make a crunchy crust.

**5** Stand the panettone pudding in a roasting pan and half-fill it with boiling water. Bake in a preheated oven, 350°F, for 25 minutes or until the custard is set.

4 tablespoons butter
5 slices of panettone
apricot preserves, for
  spreading
1 cup milk
1 cup whipping cream
2 eggs
1 egg yolk
¼ cup brown sugar, plus extra
  for the crust

Serves **4**
Prep time **5 minutes**
Cooking time **25 minutes**

# DEEP DISH PUFF APPLE PIE

2 lb or about 5 cooking apples, quartered, cored, peeled, and thickly sliced
½ cup superfine sugar, plus extra for sprinkling
grated zest of 1 small orange
½ teaspoon ground allspice or ground cinnamon
3 whole cloves
13 oz chilled puff pastry
beaten egg, to glaze
sour cream or whipping cream, to serve

Serves **6**
Prep time **40 minutes**
Cooking time **20-25 minutes**

1 Fill a 5-cup pie dish with the apple slices. Mix the sugar with the orange zest, allspice or cinnamon, and cloves and sprinkle over the apples.

2 Roll out the pastry on a lightly floured surface until it is a little larger than the top of the dish. Cut two long strips from the edges, about ½ inch wide. Brush the dish rim with a little beaten egg, press the strips on top, then brush these with egg. Lift the remaining pastry over the dish and press the edges together well.

3 Trim off the excess pastry, knock up the edges with a small knife, then flute the edges by pinching the layers of pastry between your fingers and thumb. Re-roll the trimmings and cut out small heart shapes or circles with a small cookie cutter. Brush the top of the pie with beaten egg, add the pastry shapes, and brush these with egg. Sprinkle with a little extra sugar.

4 Bake in a preheated oven, 400°F, for 20-25 minutes until the pastry is well risen and golden. Serve warm with spoonfuls of sour cream or extra-thick cream.

AFFORDABILITY
1

### Stick the knife in

It's better to have one sharp knife than a whole block of blunt ones. A good all-round chopping knife is essential for quick food preparation.

# PUMPKIN
# PIE

1 Lightly grease a 9-inch x 1-inch deep enamel pie dish. Cook the pumpkin or butternut squash in a covered steamer for 15-20 minutes until tender. Cool, then puree in a blender or food processor.

2 Beat the eggs, sugar, flour, and spices together in a bowl until just mixed. Add the pumpkin puree and beat together. Gradually mix in the milk and set aside.

3 Roll out three-quarters of the pastry on a lightly floured surface until it is large enough to line the pie dish. Lift the pastry over the rolling pin and press it over the base and sides of the dish. Trim off the excess around the rim and add the trimmings to the reserved pastry. Roll this out thinly and cut leaves, then mark veins. Brush the rim of the pastry in the dish, then press on the leaves, reserving a few. Stand the dish on a cookie sheet.

4 Pour the pumpkin filling into the dish, add a few leaves, if desired, on top of the filling, and brush these and the dish edges lightly with milk. Bake in a preheated oven, 375°F, for 45-55 minutes until the filling is set and the pastry is cooked through. Cover with kitchen foil after 20 minutes to stop the pastry edge from over-browning.

5 Serve dusted with a little confectioners' sugar and with whipped cream sprinkled with a little extra ground spice, if desired.

unsalted butter, for greasing
4 cups peeled and cubed pumpkin or butternut squash (1 lb)
3 eggs
½ cup light brown sugar
2 tablespoons all-purpose flour
½ teaspoon ground cinnamon
½ teaspoon ground ginger
¼ teaspoon grated nutmeg
scant 1 cup milk, plus extra for glazing
14½ oz chilled sweet shortcrust pastry
flour, for dusting

**To serve**
confectioners' sugar
whipped cream
ground spice

Serves **6**
Prep time **30 minutes**
Cooking time **1-1¼ hours**

# BANOFFEE PIE

¼ lb plus 6 tablespoons (1¾ sticks)
  unsalted butter, plus extra for
  greasing
2 tablespoons light corn syrup
3 cups crushed graham crackers
½ cup dark brown sugar
1 13-oz can full-fat condensed milk
1¼ cups whipping cream
3 small ripe bananas
¼ cup lemon juice
grated semisweet chocolate, to
  decorate

Serves **6**
Prep time **35 minutes, plus
chilling and cooling**
Cooking time **8 minutes**

**1** Lightly grease an 8-inch springform cake pan with some of
the unsalted butter.

**2** Melt half the butter and the syrup in a saucepan, add the
cracker crumbs and mix well. Tip into the cake pan and press
evenly over the base and up the sides almost to the top. Chill.

**3** Heat the remaining butter and the sugar in a nonstick
skillet until the butter has melted and the sugar has
dissolved. Add the condensed milk and cook over a medium
heat, stirring continuously, for 4-5 minutes until the mixture
thickens and it begins to smell of caramel. (Don't have the heat
too high or the condensed milk will burn.)

**4** Take the pan off the heat and allow the mixture to cool for
1-2 minutes. Pour it into the crumb crust, then allow to
cool completely and chill for at least 1 hour.

**5** Just before serving whip the cream until it forms soft
peaks. Halve the bananas lengthwise, then slice them and
toss them in the lemon juice. Fold two-thirds into the cream,
then spoon over the toffee layer. Arrange the remaining
bananas on top. Loosen the edge of the crumb crust with a
spatula, remove the pan and transfer the pie to a serving plate.
Sprinkle with grated chocolate and serve cut into wedges.

# *Key* LIME PIE

6 tablespoons unsalted butter, melted, plus extra for greasing
2⅓ cups crushed graham crackers
¼ cup superfine sugar
3 eggs, separated
1 13-oz can full-fat condensed milk
½ cup lime juice
1 tablespoon lemon juice
2 teaspoons grated lime zest

**Topping**
1 cup whipping cream
1 tablespoon confectioners' sugar
vanilla extract
lime slices, to decorate (optional)

Serves **8**
Prep time **30 minutes, plus chilling**
Cooking time **15-20 minutes**

**1** Lightly grease a 9-inch springform cake pan with some of the unsalted butter.

**2** Mix together the cracker crumbs, butter, and half the sugar and press the mixture over the bottom and up the sides of the cake pan. Refrigerate.

**3** Beat the egg yolks lightly together until creamy. Add the condensed milk, lime and lemon juice, and lime zest and beat until well mixed and slightly thickened. In another bowl beat the egg whites until stiff. Add the remainder of the sugar and continue beating until the meringue holds soft peaks. Use a large metal spoon to fold the meringue mixture gently but thoroughly into the lime mixture.

**4** Spoon the filling into the crust and smooth the top. Bake in a preheated oven, 325°F, for 15-20 minutes or until the filling is just firm and lightly browned on top. Cool, then refrigerate for at least 3 hours.

**5** Before serving whip the cream until it begins to thicken. Add the confectioners' sugar and vanilla extract and continue whipping until it forms thick swirls. Spread the cream over the top of the chilled pie. Decorate with twisted lime slices, if desired. Remove the side of the cake pan just before serving and serve well chilled.

# Quick
## TIRAMISU

AFFORDABILITY 3

**1** Mix the coffee with 2 tablespoons sugar and the liqueur or brandy in a bowl. Toss the ladyfingers in the mixture and arrange in a serving dish, spooning over any excess liquid.

**2** Beat together the custard, mascarpone, and vanilla extract and spoon one-third over the ladyfingers. Sprinkle with the remaining sugar, then half the remaining custard. Sprinkle with the chocolate, then spread with the remaining custard.

**3** Chill for about 1 hour until the tiramisu is set. Serve dusted with cocoa powder.

¼ cup plus 1 tablespoon strong espresso coffee
⅓ cup dark brown sugar
¼ cup coffee liqueur or 3 tablespoons brandy
9 ladyfingers, about 3 oz, broken into large pieces
1⅔ cups good-quality prepared custard
1 cup mascarpone cheese
1 teaspoon vanilla extract
2 oz semisweet chocolate, finely chopped
unsweetened cocoa powder, for dusting

Serves **4-6**
Prep time **15 minutes, plus chilling**

# *Spanish* CUSTARD CREAMS

THESE CREAMY CINNAMON-FLAVORED CUSTARDS, KNOWN AS NATILLAS IN SPAIN, ARE PERFECT TO FOLLOW A SPICY MAIN COURSE. YOU CAN ADD FINELY GRATED ORANGE OR LEMON ZEST TO THE MIXTURE FOR ADDED FLAVOR IF YOU LIKE.

3 cups low-fat milk
1 cinnamon stick
6 egg yolks
¾ cup unrefined superfine sugar
2 teaspoons cornstarch
ground cinnamon, for dusting
sweet cookies, to serve (optional)

Serves **4**
Prep time **15 minutes, plus chilling**
Cooking time **10 minutes**

1 Put all but 3 tablespoons of the milk in a saucepan, add the cinnamon stick, and bring to a boil over a medium heat.

2 Meanwhile, beat the egg yolks and sugar with an electric hand beater in a large bowl until light and frothy.

3 Blend the cornstarch with the remaining milk and add to the egg yolk mixture. Beat well to combine.

4 When the milk comes to a boil, remove from the heat and remove the cinnamon stick. Gradually add the egg mixture, stirring constantly, and then return the pan to a low heat and cook, stirring constantly, until the custard thickens. Remove from the heat and allow to cool before spooning into individual bowls or dessert glasses.

5 Cover and chill for 2-3 hours or overnight. Lightly dust with ground cinnamon before serving with sweet cookies, if desired.

# SUMMER BERRY **SORBET**

**AFFORDABILITY 1**

1 Put a shallow plastic container into the freezer to chill ready for the sorbet.

2 Whiz the frozen berries, cordial, Kirsch, and lime juice in a food processor or blender to give a smooth puree. Take care not to over-process the puree because this will soften the mixture too much.

3 Spoon the sorbet into the chilled container and freeze for at least 25 minutes. Spoon into bowls and serve.

1½ cups frozen mixed summer berries
⅓ cup spiced berry cordial
2 tablespoons Kirsch
1 tablespoon lime juice

Serves **2**
Prep time **5 minutes**
Freezing time **25 minutes**

CHUNKY POTATO FRIES

ROASTED TOMATO SAUCE

GRAVY

GLOSSY CHOCOLATE SAUCE

# BACK TO BASICS

# GRAVY

GOOD-QUALITY CUTS OF ROASTED MEAT OR POULTRY PROVIDE DELICIOUS FATS AND JUICES FOR A WELL-FLAVORED GRAVY. AFTER ROASTING, DRAIN THE MEAT, COVER IT LOOSELY WITH KITCHEN FOIL AND MAKE THE GRAVY WHILE THE MEAT STANDS.

pan juices from roasted meat
1 tablespoon all-purpose flour (less for a thin gravy)
1¼-1²/₃ cups liquid (this could be water, drained from the accompanying vegetables; stock; half stock and half water; or half wine and half water)
salt and pepper

Makes **about 2½ cups**
Cooking time **5 minutes**

1 Tilt the roasting pan and skim off the fat from the surface with a large serving spoon until you are left with the pan juices and just a thin layer of fat.

2 Sprinkle the flour into the pan and stir with a wooden spoon over a moderate heat, scraping up all the residue, particularly from around the edges.

3 Gradually pour the liquid into the pan, stirring well until the gravy is thick and glossy. Let the mixture bubble, then check the seasoning, adding a little salt and pepper if necessary.

# CREAMY **BREAD** SAUCE

1 Peel the onions but leave them whole and stud them with the cloves. Put them in a saucepan with the milk and bay leaves and bring the milk almost to a boil. Reduce the heat and cook on the lowest setting for 10 minutes to let the flavors infuse the milk.

2 Remove the onions from the saucepan and add the bread crumbs, butter, peppercorns, and plenty of grated nutmeg. Cook gently for 5 minutes until the sauce is thick and pulpy.

3 Stir in the cream and season with salt and pepper to taste. Serve hot sprinkled with extra grated nutmeg, if desired.

2 onions
8 whole cloves
scant 2 cups whole milk
2 bay leaves
3 cups fresh white bread crumbs
2 tablespoons butter
1 tablespoon green peppercorns in brine, drained and lightly crushed
grated nutmeg
3 tablespoons cream
salt

Serves **8**
Prep time **10 minutes, plus infusing**
Cooking time **15 minutes**

# **BÉCHAMEL** SAUCE

1 Put the milk in a saucepan with the onion, bay leaf, peppercorns, and parsley stalks and bring almost to a boil. Remove the pan from the heat and allow to infuse for 20 minutes. Strain the milk through a sieve into a pitcher.

2 Melt the butter in a heavy saucepan until bubbling. Tip in the flour and stir quickly to combine. Cook the mixture gently, stirring constantly with a wooden spoon, for 1-2 minutes to make a smooth, pale roux.

3 Remove the pan from the heat and gradually beat in the warm milk, stirring constantly until the sauce is completely smooth. Return the pan to a moderate heat and cook, stirring, until the sauce comes to a boil.

4 Reduce the heat to low and continue to cook the sauce for about 5 minutes, stirring frequently until it is smooth and glossy and thinly coats the back of the spoon. Season to taste with salt, pepper, and plenty of grated nutmeg.

1¼ cups whole milk
½ small onion
1 bay leaf
½ teaspoon peppercorns
3-4 parsley stalks
1 tablespoon butter
2 tablespoons all-purpose flour
pinch of grated nutmeg
salt and pepper

Serves **4**
Prep time **10 minutes, plus infusing**
Cooking time **10 minutes**

# RICH
## CHEESE
## SAUCE

1¼ cups whole milk
½ small onion
1 bay leaf
1 tablespoon butter
2 tablespoons all-purpose flour
1 teaspoon green peppercorns in
  brine, rinsed and drained
¾ cup grated sharp cheddar
  cheese
2 tablespoons grated Parmesan
  cheese
pinch of grated nutmeg
salt

Serves **4**
Prep time **10 minutes**
Cooking time **10 minutes**

THIS SMOOTH, CREAMY SAUCE IS SIMPLE AND DELICIOUS AND IDEAL FOR USING UP LEFTOVER CHEESE. YOU CAN VARY THE RECIPE WITH PIECES OF GRUYERE OR STILTON OR EVEN COMBINE SEVERAL CHEESES.

1 Follow steps 1, 2, and 3 of Béchamel Sauce (see page 223) but omit the black peppercorns and parsley.

2 Lightly crush the green peppercorns in a mortar and pestle until they are broken into small pieces. Add them to the sauce with the cheeses and a little nutmeg. Cook over a gentle heat, stirring frequently, for about 5 minutes until smooth and glossy. Check the seasoning and serve hot.

# APPLESAUCE

A CLASSIC ACCOMPANIMENT TO ROAST PORK AND GOOSE, APPLESAUCE IS
ALSO DELICIOUS WITH CHICKEN, LAMB, DUCK, GAME, AND OTHER RICH,
FATTY MEATS.

1 Melt the butter in a heavy saucepan. Add the apples,
sugar, cloves, lemon zest and juice, and a small pinch
of salt.

2 Cover the pan with a lid and allow to cook gently over
the lowest heat for about 20 minutes, stirring the
mixture occasionally, until the apples are very soft and
mushy. Check the seasoning, adding a little more lemon
juice for a tangier flavor, if desired. Transfer to a sauce boat
and serve warm or cold.

4 tablespoons unsalted butter
3 large cooking apples, peeled,
  cored, and chopped
¼ cup sugar
6 whole cloves
finely grated zest and juice of 1
  lemon
salt

Serves **6**
Prep time **10 minutes**
Cooking time **20 minutes**

# **MINT** SAUCE

THIS CLASSIC SAUCE GOES WITH PAN-FRIED DUCK BREASTS AS WELL AS GRILLED
AND ROAST LAMB. DON'T THROW AWAY ANY LEFTOVER MINT SAUCE AFTER
A LAMB DINNER—ADD A SPLASH OF OLIVE OIL AND SERVE IT AS A DRESSING
FOR WARM NEW POTATOES OR DRIZZLE OVER PEAS OR SNOW PEAS.

1 Pull the mint leaves from their stalks and chop the
leaves finely.

2 Put the mint in a small bowl with the sugar and the
boiling water. Allow to infuse for 5 minutes, stirring
once or twice until the sugar dissolves.

3 Add the vinegar and allow to stand for about 1 hour
before serving.

3 tablespoons mint
1 tablespoon sugar
1 tablespoon boiling water
2 tablespoons white wine vinegar

Serves **6**
Prep time **10 minutes, plus
infusing**

# SATAY
# SAUCE

THIS SAUCE IS DELICIOUSLY RICH, SPICY, AND PEANUTTY AND SERVES SEVERAL DIFFERENT PURPOSES. IT IS GENERALLY USED AS A MAIN MEAL ACCOMPANIMENT, BUT IT'S ALSO GOOD AS A DIPPING SAUCE, SERVED ON A PLATTER WITH A SELECTION OF VEGETABLES OR SMALL PIECES OF SKEWERED CHICKEN, PORK, OR FISH.

1 lemon grass stalk
1 small onion, chopped
2 garlic cloves, chopped
1 teaspoon shrimp paste or Thai fish sauce (nam pla)
1 teaspoon tamarind paste
1 hot red chile, seeded and chopped
1 tablespoon light brown sugar
scant 1 cup coconut milk
¾ cup smooth or crunchy peanut butter
1 tablespoon soy sauce

Serves **4-6**
Prep time **10 minutes**
Cooking time **7 minutes**

**1** Trim the ends from the lemon grass and remove any coarse or damaged outer leaves. Cut the stalk into thin slices.

**2** Put the lemon grass, onion, garlic, shrimp paste or fish sauce, tamarind paste, and chile into a food processor or blender. Add 2 tablespoons water and the sugar and blend to a paste, scraping down the mixture from the sides of the bowl with a spatula if necessary.

**3** Transfer the mixture to a saucepan with the coconut milk. Bring almost to a boil (watching closely so the coconut milk does not boil over), then reduce the heat and simmer gently for 5 minutes.

**4** Add the peanut butter and soy sauce and cook very gently for 2 minutes or until the sauce is heated through and thickened. Check the seasoning, adding a dash more soy sauce, if desired, and more coconut milk if the sauce is too thick. Transfer to a serving bowl and serve warm.

# ROASTED
# TOMATO
# SAUCE

**1** Halve the tomatoes and arrange them, cut sides up, in a large, shallow, heatproof dish or roasting pan. Drizzle with 2 tablespoons oil, the sugar, and seasoning. Roast in a preheated oven, 400°F, for 40 minutes or until the tomatoes are soft and beginning to color.

**2** Gently fry the onion in the remaining oil in a saucepan for about 10 minutes or until it is soft, adding the garlic for the last couple of minutes. Blend the tomatoes in a food processor or blender and add to the pan with the oregano.

**3** Cook gently for 5–10 minutes or until slightly thickened. Check the seasoning and serve.

2 lb very ripe tomatoes
¼ cup olive oil
1 teaspoon sugar
1 onion, finely chopped
4 garlic cloves, crushed
2 tablespoons chopped oregano
salt and pepper

Makes **750 ml (1¼ pints)**
Prep time **10 minutes**
Cooking time **50 minutes**

# PESTO

MAKING PESTO WITH A MORTAR AND PESTLE FILLS THE AIR WITH THE
WONDERFUL FRAGRANCE OF CRUSHED BASIL LEAVES BUT IS MORE TIME
CONSUMING THAN THE QUICK AND EASY FOOD PROCESSOR METHOD USED
HERE. FRESHLY MADE PESTO HAS NUMEROUS USES, MOST COMMONLY AS
A PASTA SAUCE BUT ALSO TO FLAVOR SOUPS, STEWS, AND RISOTTOS.

⅔ cup basil, including stalks
⅓ cup pine nuts
generous ½ cup grated
   Parmesan cheese
2 garlic cloves, chopped
½ cup olive oil
salt

Serves **4**
Prep time **5 minutes**

**1** Tear the basil into pieces and put them into a food processor
with the pine nuts, Parmesan, and garlic.

**2** Blend lightly until the nuts and cheese are broken into
small pieces, scraping the mixture down from the sides of
the bowl with a spatula if necessary.

**3** Add the olive oil and a little salt and blend to a thick paste.
It can be kept, covered, in the refrigerator for up to 5 days.

# *Fresh* HERB BUTTER

RICH AND DELICIOUS, FLAVORED BUTTERS MAKE SOME OF THE BEST AND SIMPLEST SAUCES AS THEY MELT OVER GRILLED, BAKED, OR PAN-FRIED MEAT OR FISH. THEY'RE EASY TO MAKE, CAN BE PREPARED AHEAD AND EVEN FROZEN.

1 Put the butter in a small bowl with the salt, parsley, chives, lemon juice, and several grinds of black pepper. (Unsalted butter is best, but if you only have salted, leave out the additional salt.)

2 Beat the mixture together with a wooden spoon until evenly combined.

3 If you are not using the butter immediately it can be shaped into a roll and chilled for up to 2 days, or frozen for several weeks, a worthwhile way of using up a large quantity of fresh herbs. Simply turn the mixture onto a strip of waxed paper and bring the sides of the paper up over the butter, gently squeezing it into a sausage shape about 1¼ inches in diameter. Chill or freeze the butter until you are ready to use it. If it is frozen leave it at room temperature for 20-30 minutes before serving.

7 tablespoons unsalted butter, softened
¼ teaspoon salt
2 tablespoons finely chopped parsley
2 tablespoons finely snipped chives
2 teaspoons lemon juice
pepper

Serves **4-6**
Prep time **3 minutes, plus chilling**

# CHUNKY
## POTATO FRIES

THIS IS THE NO-FUSS VERSION OF TRADITIONAL FRIES. THEY ARE SIMPLE TO MAKE—
YOU CAN POP THEM IN THE OVEN AND FORGET ABOUT THEM (UNLIKE
TRADITIONAL FRIES)—AND ARE A GOOD ACCOMPANIMENT TO PAN-FRIED, BAKED, OR
GRILLED FISH.

2 lb baking potatoes
2/3 cup mild olive oil or peanut oil
1 teaspoon paprika
1 teaspoon celery salt
salt and pepper

Serves **4**
Prep time **10 minutes**
Cooking time **50 minutes**

 **1** Cut the potatoes into ½-inch slices, then cut each slice into chunky fries.

**2** Brush a large roasting pan with a little of the oil and heat it in a preheated oven, 425°F, for 5 minutes.

**3** Place the fries in the pan, drizzle with the remaining oil, and sprinkle with the paprika and celery salt. Mix until well coated and bake for 45 minutes, turning the fries occasionally, until they are golden. Serve sprinkled with salt and pepper.

# BOILED RICE

1 Put the rice in a fine-mesh strainer and wash it under running warm water, rubbing the grains together between your hands to get rid of any excess starch.

2 Put the rice into a saucepan and add the stock. Set the pan on the smallest ring on the stovetop and bring it to a boil. Give it a quick stir then reduce the heat to a simmer. Cover with a lid and allow to cook for 15 minutes. Turn off the heat and allow the rice to steam with the lid on for another 20 minutes. Don't be tempted to lift the lid to check what's going on.

3 To serve fluff up the grains of rice with a spoon or fork.

1¾ cups Thai jasmine or long grain rice
1¼ cups Vegetable or Chicken Stock (see pages 234 and 235)

Serves **4**
Prep time **10 minutes**
Cooking time **40 minutes**

# YORKSHIRE PUDDINGS

1 To make the batter, sift the flour and salt into a large bowl and make a well in the center. Add the milk or milk and water and beat until smooth and bubbly. Beat the eggs in a clean bowl, then fold quickly into the batter. Allow to stand for 30 minutes.

2 Pour ½ teaspoon oil into each of 12 deep muffin cups and place in a preheated oven, 425°F, for 5 minutes until very hot. Quickly pour the batter into the cups to half-fill them, return them to the oven, and bake for about 20 minutes until well risen, crisp, and golden brown.

1 cup all-purpose flour
pinch of salt
⅔ cup milk or half milk and half water
2 eggs
oil, for greasing

Makes **12**
Prep time **10 minutes, plus standing**
Cooking time **20-25 minutes**

# OMELET

2 eggs
1 tablespoon butter
salt and pepper

Serves **1**
Prep time **2 minutes**
Cooking time **3-4 minutes**

1 Break the eggs into a bowl and beat lightly with an egg whisk. Beat in 1 tablespoon water and season well with salt and pepper. Do not over-beat because this will ruin the texture of the finished omelet.

2 Set a skillet over a gentle heat and, when it is hot, add the butter. Tip the pan so that the entire inner surface is coated with butter. When the butter is foaming, but not browned, tip in the eggs.

3 Leave for a few seconds then, using a spatula, draw the mixture away from the edge of the pan into the center, allowing the eggs to run to the sides. Repeat the process twice more, by which time the eggs should have set. Cook for another 30 seconds until the underside is golden and top still slightly runny and creamy. Tilt the pan and, with the spatula, carefully turn the omelet onto a plate, folding it in half in the process.

## Grow your own ...

... cooking herbs that is! You don't need a big yard—or any outside space for that matter—to grow some essential herbs. For the price of a few plastic containers and packets of seeds, you could have your own collection of basil, parsley, and mint, ready to add another level to boring soups and sauces.

# CRUSHED MINTED **PEAS**

*A COMPULSORY ACCOMPANIMENT TO THE BEST FISH AND CHIPS.*

1 Cook the peas with the mint in a large saucepan of lightly salted boiling water for about 5 minutes or until tender. Drain and return to the pan, discarding the mint.

2 Stir in the butter and sour cream and use a potato masher to crush the peas roughly. Season to taste with salt and pepper and reheat gently.

2²/₃ cups peas, shelled
several mint sprigs
2 tablespoons butter
2 tablespoons sour cream
salt and pepper

Serves **4-6**
Prep time **10 minutes**
Cooking time **5 minutes**

# **ROASTED** VEGETABLE & **HERB** COUSCOUS

1 Put the pumpkin, zucchini, and onion in a roasting pan with 2 tablespoons oil, season to taste with salt and pepper, and stir to combine.

2 Roast in a preheated oven, 425°F, for 25 minutes until all the vegetables are cooked.

3 Meanwhile, put the couscous in a heatproof bowl and pour over the water. Cover the bowl with a clean dish towel and allow to stand for 5 minutes or until the grains are swollen and all the liquid has been absorbed.

4 Fluff up the couscous with a fork, then stir in the roasted vegetables, cherry tomatoes, and herbs.

5 Beat together the remaining oil, the lemon juice, and salt and pepper to taste in a small bowl and stir through the salad.

4 cups peeled and diced
    pumpkin
4 zucchini, diced
1 red onion, cut into wedges
1/3 cup extra virgin olive oil
generous 1 cup couscous
1 cup boiling water
1 cup cherry tomatoes, halved
2 tablespoons each chopped
    fresh cilantro, mint, and
    parsley
juice of 1 large lemon
salt and pepper

Serves **6**
Prep time **15 minutes, plus
soaking**
Cooking time **25 minutes**

# BEEF STOCK

WHEN YOU BUY A PIECE OF BEEF, GET THE BONES AS WELL AND ASK THE BUTCHER TO CUT THEM INTO PIECES. FOR A RICHLY COLORED STOCK, YOU CAN ROAST THE BONES IN A PREHEATED OVEN, 400°F, FOR 45 MINUTES BEFOREHAND.

1½ lb beef bones
1 large onion, unpeeled and
    quartered
1 large carrot, coarsely chopped
2 celery sticks, coarsely chopped
1 bouquet garni
1 teaspoon black peppercorns

Makes **about 4 cups**
Prep time **10 minutes**
Cooking time **3 hours**

**1** Put the bones into a large, heavy saucepan with the onion, carrot, celery, bouquet garni, and peppercorns. Add 7½ cups cold water and bring slowly to a boil.

**2** Reduce the heat and simmer the stock very gently for 3 hours, skimming the surface from time to time if necessary.

**3** Strain the stock through a large strainer, preferably a conical one, and allow to cool. Don't squeeze the juice out of the vegetables or the stock will be cloudy.

**4** Allow the stock to cool completely, then chill. Remove any layer of fat that might have set on the surface before use.

# LAMB STOCK

**1** See the above recipe and simply substitute the beef bones for leftover lamb bones (roast them first for a darker stock), and simmer for just 1½ hours.

# CHICKEN STOCK

1 large chicken carcass, plus any
    trimmings
giblets, except the liver, if available
1 onion, quartered
1 celery stick, coarsely chopped
1 bouquet garni or 3 bay leaves
1 teaspoon black peppercorns

Makes **about 4 cups**
Prep time **10 minutes**
Cooking time **1½ hours**

IDEALLY CHICKEN STOCK IS MADE USING A RAW CARCASS, BUT A COOKED CARCASS ALSO MAKES A WELL-FLAVORED STOCK THAT MIGHT JUST BE A LITTLE CLOUDY.

**1** Put the chicken carcass, giblets, onion, celery, bouquet garni, and peppercorns into a large, heavy saucepan and add 7½ cups cold water.

**2** Make the stock following the recipe for Beef Stock (see above) but simmer it for just 1½ hours.

# VEGETABLE STOCK

THE VEGETABLES CAN VARY BUT MAKE SURE YOU INCLUDE SOME ONION AND OMIT VEGETABLES WITH STRONG FLAVORS AND STARCHY ONES LIKE POTATOES. FOR A DARK STOCK, LEAVE THE SKINS ON THE ONIONS AND USE PLENTY OF MUSHROOMS.

1 Heat the oil in a large, heavy saucepan and gently fry all the vegetables for 5 minutes.

2 Add 6¼ cups cold water, then follow the method for Beef Stock (see opposite), but simmering the stock for just 40 minutes.

1 tablespoon sunflower oil
2 onions, coarsely chopped
2 carrots, coarsely chopped
2 celery sticks, coarsely chopped
1 lb mixture of other vegetables (such as parsnips, fennel, leeks, zucchini, mushrooms, and tomatoes), coarsely chopped
1 bouquet garni
1 teaspoon black peppercorns

Makes **about 4 cups**
Prep time **10 minutes**
Cooking time **45 minutes**

# FISH STOCK

DON'T USE OILY FISH IN A STOCK—IT WILL MAKE IT GREASY AND GIVE IT AN OVERPOWERING FLAVOR.

1 Melt the butter in a large, heavy saucepan until bubbling. Add all the vegetables and fry gently for 5 minutes to soften them slightly but without browning.

2 Add the fish bones, wine, parsley, lemon slices, peppercorns, and 4 cups cold water.

3 Follow the method for Beef Stock (see opposite), but simmering the stock for just 20 minutes.

2 tablespoons butter
3 shallots, coarsely chopped
1 small leek, coarsely chopped
1 celery stick or piece of fennel, coarsely chopped
2 lb white fish or shellfish bones, heads, and scraps
⅔ cup dry white wine
several parsley stalks
½ lemon, sliced
1 teaspoon black or white peppercorns

Makes **about 4 cups**
Prep time **5 minutes**
Cooking time **25 minutes**

# Glossy
## **CHOCOLATE** SAUCE

A GOOD CHOCOLATE SAUCE SHOULD BE SMOOTH AND GLOSSY AND TASTE ALMOST LIKE PURE MELTED CHOCOLATE. USE A GOOD-QUALITY DARK CHOCOLATE WITH ABOUT 70 PER CENT COCOA SOLIDS TO GIVE A RICH FLAVOR AND PLENTY OF SHEEN. TAKE CARE NOT TO OVERHEAT THE CHOCOLATE OR THE SAUCE WILL DEVELOP A GRAINY TEXTURE.

generous ½ cup superfine sugar
7 oz bittersweet chocolate,
   chopped
2 tablespoons unsalted butter

Serves **5-6**
Prep time **5 minutes**
Cooking time **2-3 minutes**

**1** Put the sugar in a small, heavy saucepan and add ½ cup water. Cook over a low heat, stirring constantly with a wooden spoon, until the sugar has dissolved.

**2** Bring the syrup to a boil and boil for 1 minute, then remove the pan from the heat and allow to cool for 1 minute. Tip the chocolate into the pan.

**3** Add the butter and leave until the chocolate and butter have melted, stirring frequently, until the sauce is smooth and glossy. If the last of the chocolate doesn't melt completely or you want to serve the sauce warm, return the pan briefly to the lowest heat setting.

# Custard

SMOOTH, CREAMY, AND COMFORTING, CUSTARD IS ALWAYS A GREAT FAVORITE AND WELL WORTH THE EFFORT OF MAKING FROM SCRATCH.

1 Put the vanilla bean into a heavy saucepan with the milk and cream and bring slowly to a boil. Remove from the heat and allow to infuse for 15 minutes.

2 Beat together the egg yolks and sugar in a bowl with an egg whisk until thick and pale. Lift the vanilla bean out of the pan and scrape the seeds into the pan.

3 Pour the milk over the creamed mixture, beating well. Return the mixture to a clean pan and cook over a medium heat, stirring constantly with a wooden spoon, until the sauce thickly coats the back of the spoon. This will take about 5-10 minutes, but don't be tempted to increase the heat or the custard might curdle. Serve warm.

1 vanilla bean, split lengthwise
1¼ cups whole milk
1¼ cups light cream
6 egg yolks
2 tablespoons superfine sugar

Serves **6**
Prep time **10 minutes, plus infusing**
Cooking time **10-15 minutes**

MULLED WINE

BLOODY MARY

# BLOODY MARY

THE LEGENDARY FERNAND PETOIT, OF THE FAMOUS HARRY'S BAR IN PARIS, WAS THE INVENTOR OF THE BLOODY MARY.

ice cubes
2 measures vodka
1 dash lemon juice
Worcestershire sauce, to taste
tomato juice, to top up
½ teaspoon cayenne pepper
salt and pepper
tomato and celery sticks, to decorate

**1** Put some ice cubes into a highball glass.

**2** Pour over the vodka and lemon juice, add Worcestershire sauce to taste and top up with tomato juice. Add the cayenne pepper and season to taste with salt and pepper. Stir to chill. Decorate with a tomato and celery sticks and serve.

Serves **1**
Prep time **2 minutes**

# BAY Breeze

THIS IS A VARIATION OF THE CLASSIC SEA BREEZE (SEE OPPOSITE). HERE, PINEAPPLE JUICE IS USED TO ADD A TOUCH OF SWEETNESS THAT CONTRASTS WITH THE PIQUANT FLAVOR OF CRANBERRIES.

ice cubes
4 measures cranberry juice
2 measures vodka
2 measures pineapple juice
lime wedges, to decorate

**1** Fill a highball glass with ice cubes and pour over the cranberry juice.

**2** Pour the vodka and pineapple juice into a chilled cocktail shaker, shake well, and gently pour over the cranberry juice and ice in the glass. Decorate with lime wedges and serve with long straws.

Serves **1**
Prep time **2 minutes**

# SEA BREEZE

THIS REFRESHING CONTEMPORARY CLASSIC IS THE TANGIER SISTER DRINK TO BAY BREEZE, MADE WITH PINK GRAPEFRUIT RATHER THAN PINEAPPLE JUICE.

1 Put some ice cubes into a highball or hurricane glass.

2 Pour over the vodka and fruit juices. Squeeze the lime wedges into the drink and stir lightly before serving.

ice cubes
2 measures vodka
4 measures cranberry juice
2 measures pink grapefruit juice
2 lime wedges

Serves **1**
Prep time **2 minutes**

## Shaking

Shaking is used to mix ingredients quickly and thoroughly and to chill the drink before serving.

Half-fill the cocktail shaker or the Boston glass (if using a Boston shaker) with ice cubes (or the amount specified in the recipe) or add cracked or crushed ice. If the recipe calls for a chilled glass, add a few ice cubes and some water to the glass and swirl them around before discarding. Add the remaining ingredients to the shaker. Put on the strainer and cap or, if using a Boston shaker, place the metal tumbler over the glass. Shake until condensation forms on the outside of the shaker. Use both hands to hold either end of the shaker and to prevent it from slipping from your grip. The cocktail is then ready to be strained into the glass for serving by removing the cap but keeping the strainer in place.

# MOSCOW MULE

THIS WAS INVENTED IN 1941 BY AN EMPLOYEE OF A U.S. DRINKS FIRM IN CONJUNCTION WITH A LOS ANGELES BAR OWNER WHO WAS OVERSTOCKED WITH GINGER BEER

1 Put the cracked ice into a cocktail shaker. Add the vodka and lime juice and shake until a frost forms on the outside of the shaker.

2 Pour, without straining, into a highball glass, top up with ginger beer, and stir lightly. Decorate with lime or orange wheels and serve.

3-4 ice cubes, cracked
2 measures vodka
juice of 2 limes
ginger beer, to top up
lime or orange wheels, to decorate

Serves **1**
Prep time **2 minutes**

# BLACK RUSSIAN

THIS IS THE ORIGINAL COCKTAIL, DATING BACK TO THE 1950s. NOWADAYS, IT IS OFTEN SERVED AS A LONG DRINK, TOPPED UP WITH CHILLED COLA.

4-6 ice cubes, cracked
2 measures vodka
1 measure Kahlúa
chocolate stick, to decorate
    (optional)

1 Put the cracked ice into a rocks (old-fashioned) glass. Pour over the vodka and Kahlúa and stir.

2 Decorate with a chocolate stick, if you desire, and serve.

Serves **1**
Prep time **2 minutes**

# WHITE RUSSIAN

THIS MODERN TAKE ON THE BLACK RUSSIAN USES TIA MARIA AND CREAM TO GIVE THE DRINK ITS DISTINCTIVE COLOR AND TEXTURE.

6 ice cubes, cracked
1 measure vodka
1 measure Tia Maria
1 measure whole milk or
    whipping cream

1 Put half the cracked ice into a cocktail shaker and put the remaining cracked ice into a highball glass.

2 Add all the remaining ingredients to the shaker and shake until a frost forms on the outside of the shaker. Strain over the ice in the glass. Serve with a straw.

Serves **1**
Prep time **2 minutes**

## Muddling

This is the technique used to bring out the flavors of fruit and herbs using a blunt tool called a muddler. A famous example is the Mojito, where mint, sugar syrup, and lime wedges are muddled in the bottom of a highball glass before the remaining ingredients are added.

Remove the mint leaves from their stems and put them into the bottom of a highball glass. Add the sugar syrup and lime wedges. Hold the glass firmly with one hand and use the muddler to press down on the mint and lime wedges. Twist the muddler and press firmly to release the flavor of the mint and to break it down with the juice from the lime wedges. Continue this process for about 30 seconds, then top up the glass with crushed ice. Add the remaining ingredients to the glass, as specified in the recipe.

# MOJITO

THIS IS A COOLING, EFFERVESCENT COCKTAIL BORN— THANKS TO PROHIBITION—AMID CUBA'S THRIVING INTERNATIONAL BAR CULTURE. IT PROBABLY DERIVED FROM THE MINT JULEP.

12 mint leaves, plus an extra
  sprig to decorate
½ measure sugar syrup (see
  page 245)
4 lime wedges
crushed ice
2 measures white rum
soda water, to top up

1 Put the mint, sugar syrup, and lime wedges into a highball glass and muddle together (see left).

2 Fill the glass with crushed ice, pour over the rum, and stir. Top up with soda water. Decorate with a mint sprig and serve with straws.

Serves **1**
Prep time **2 minutes**

# *Rusty* NAIL

AN AFTER-DINNER DRINK WHOSE NAME IS PROBABLY DUE TO ITS COLOR RATHER THAN IMMIGRANT SCOTTISH BARTENDERS STIRRING THE COCKTAIL WITH A RUSTY NAIL BEFORE SERVING IT TO THEIR AMERICAN PATRONS, AS LEGEND HAS IT.

ice cubes
1½ measures Scotch whisky
1 measure Drambuie

1 Fill a rocks (old-fashioned) glass with ice cubes.

2 Pour over the whisky and Drambuie and serve.

Serves **1**
Prep time **2 minutes**

# DRY MARTINI

THE MOST FAMOUS COCKTAIL OF ALL WAS INVENTED AT THE KNICKERBOCKER HOTEL IN NEW YORK IN 1910. LEMON ZEST IS SOMETIMES USED AS A DECORATION INSTEAD OF A GREEN OLIVE.

5-6 ice cubes
½ measure dry vermouth
3 measures gin
green olive, to decorate

Serves **1**
Prep time **2 minutes**

**1** Put the ice cubes into a mixing glass. Pour over the vermouth and gin and stir (never shake) vigorously and evenly without splashing.

**2** Strain into a chilled Martini (cocktail) glass. Decorate with a green olive and serve.

# COSMOPOLITAN

MANY PEOPLE LAY CLAIM TO BEING THE
INVENTOR OF THE COSMOPOLITAN; HOWEVER,
IT IS A RELATIVELY RECENT COCKTAIL THAT HAS
BECOME SOMETHING OF A CLASSIC ALREADY.

**1** Put the cracked ice into a cocktail shaker. Add all the remaining ingredients and shake until a frost forms on the outside of the shaker.

**2** Strain into a chilled Martini (cocktail) glass. Decorate with an orange zest twist and serve.

6 ice cubes, cracked
1 measure vodka
½ measure Cointreau
1 measure cranberry juice
juice of ½ lime
orange zest twist, to decorate

Serves **1**
Prep time **2 minutes**

## Stirring

"Shaken or stirred?" is the usual response from a bartender when a Martini is ordered and, despite James Bond's famously declared preference, Martinis are best served stirred, not shaken. A cocktail is prepared by stirring when it must maintain clarity yet also requires the ingredients to be mixed and chilled. This ensures that there is no fragmented ice or air bubbles throughout the drink. Some stirred cocktails will require the ingredients to be prepared in a mixing glass, then strained into the serving glass with a fine strainer, while others call for the drink to be prepared and stirred in the same glass.

Add the ingredients, in the order stated in the recipe, either to the mixing glass or the serving glass. Using a bar spoon, either lightly or vigorously stir the drink, again according to the recipe. It is important to follow the recipe exactly because some drinks will require just a slight blending of the ingredients and will not benefit from over-stirring. Finish the drink with any decoration required and serve.

## Sugar syrup

This is used as a sweetener in lots of cocktails. It blends into a cold drink more quickly than sugar and adds body. You can buy it in bottles, but it's very easy to make your own. Simply bring equal quantities of sugar and water to a boil in a small saucepan, stirring continuously, then boil for 1–2 minutes without stirring. Sugar syrup can be kept in a sterilized bottle in the refrigerator for up to two months.

# HANGOVERS & DRINKING GAMES

With a bottle of gin, a bottle of vodka, and a few choice mixers, you can rustle up a whole selection of chic-sounding cocktails and transform a dull Friday night into a swish soirée. Add some nibbles and a couple of drinking games and you've got yourself a real party.

## DRINK AND THINK

Whoever starts has to call out the name of someone famous. The next in the line, or circle, must use the first letter of the last name called out for the first name of their famous person—for example, Elvis Presley could be followed by Paul McCartney and so on.

## SHOT ROULETTE

This is pretty self-explanatory. Gather together as many shot glasses as there are guests and fill them all with water, except one, which you fill with a vodka shot. Pass them around and whoever downs the vodka sits out the next round. Keep going until you have a winner.

## THE MORNING AFTER

While we advise you to drink in moderation, pace yourself, and know when it's time to go home, we know that over-indulgence can be a part of many students' lives. So, instead of going on about memory loss and the sudden desire to eat kebabs, we're here to pick up the pieces and offer some essential advice for the morning after.

## A WALK IN THE PARK

While a lie-in is the usual way to combat a thumping head, it is more beneficial to drag yourself out of bed. Fresh air and exercise will help to rid your body of the alcohol. And, if there's a café at the end of that walk, with free tea refills, so much the better.

## EAT YOUR WAY TO SOBRIETY

There's a reason why people have greasy fry-ups: the fat, salt, and carbohydrates help to speed up the recovery process. But don't forget to drink plenty of water as well.

## THINK AHEAD

It's always best to tackle a hangover before it's arrived.

- Drink a large glass of water before bed.
- Try to eat something. A piece of toast, banana, or biscuit are easy, even with blurred vision.
- Take a drink up to bed with you (non-alcoholic that is), so you can top up on fluids during the night.

# WHISKY MAC

A WARMING SLUG MADE WITH EQUAL MEASURES OF SCOTCH AND GINGER WINE, THIS IS A DELICIOUS WINTER PICK-ME-UP.

3-4 ice cubes
1 measure Scotch whisky
1 measure ginger wine

Serves **1**
Prep time **2 minutes**

1 Put the ice cubes into a rocks (old-fashioned) glass.

2 Pour over the whisky and ginger wine, stir lightly, and serve.

# MARGARITA

THE EXACT ORIGIN OF THIS FAMOUS DRINK IS UNKNOWN. ONE STORY TELLS OF A SHOWGIRL WHO WAS ALLERGIC TO ALL ALCOHOL EXCEPT TEQUILA. SHE ASKED A BARTENDER TO CREATE HER A COCKTAIL WITH THE SPIRIT AND THE REST IS HISTORY.

1 lime wedge
rock salt
ice cubes
2 measures Tequila
1 measure lime juice
1 measure triple sec
lime wheel, to decorate

Serves **1**
Prep time **2 minutes**

1 Moisten the rim of a Margarita (coupette) glass with the lime wedge and frost with the salt (see right).

2 Half-fill a cocktail shaker with ice cubes. Add all the remaining ingredients and shake until a frost forms on the outside of the shaker. Strain into the glass. Decorate with a lime wheel and serve.

## Frosting glasses

Although not strictly a decoration, this effect does add to the final look of a drink. As with some other decorations, frosting can either perform a practical function, as in the Margarita, or a purely visual one. In general, glasses are either frosted with sugar or salt, but more unusual frostings can be used to complement flavors in cocktails, such as cocoa powder with a chocolate cocktail.

Dip the rim of the glass in a small saucer of lime or lemon juice, lightly beaten egg white, or water. Spread the desired frosting on a clean work surface or on a small plate or saucer. Place the glass on the frosting, twisting slightly to ensure you get an even coating. Clean excess frosting from the inside of the glass using a lemon or lime wedge to prevent it from contaminating the cocktail.

# SANGRIA

THIS CLASSIC SPANISH PUNCH USES RED WINE AS ITS FOUNDATION. WITH THE ADDITION OF CHOPPED FRUIT AND CINNAMON, IT'S LIKE A SUMMERTIME VERSION OF MULLED WINE.

1 Put some ice cubes into a large pitcher. Add the wine, brandy, fruit wedges, and one cinnamon stick and stir well.

2 When ready to serve, top up with the chilled lemonade and stir. Serve in glasses decorated with orange, lemon, and apple wheels and cinnamon sticks.

ice cubes
2 bottles light Spanish red wine, chilled
5 measures brandy
orange, lemon, and apple wedges, plus orange, lemon, and apple wheels
cinnamon sticks
about 2 cups lemonade, chilled

Serves **10-12**
Prep time **5 minutes**

# MULLED WINE

1 Pour the wine, apple juice, 1¼ cups water, and orange juice into a large, heavy saucepan.

2 Add the sliced orange and lemon, the cinnamon stick, cloves, and bay leaves, then mix in the sugar and brandy. Heat, stirring, until the sugar has dissolved, then bring to a boil and simmer gently for 10 minutes.

3 Keep warm over a low heat and ladle into heatproof glasses to serve.

3 cups or 1 bottle inexpensive red wine
1¼ cups clear apple juice
juice of 1 orange
1 orange, sliced
½ lemon, sliced
1 cinnamon stick, halved
6 whole cloves
2 bay leaves
generous ½ cup sugar
⅔ cup brandy

Serves **6**
Prep time **5 minutes**
Cooking time **10-15 minutes**

# B-52

THIS IS THE CLASSIC LAYERED SHOT THAT TASTES JUST AS GOOD AS IT LOOKS, WITH A WONDERFUL WARM, SWEET FLAVOR.

½ measure Kahlúa
½ measure Baileys Irish Cream
½ measure Grand Marnier

Serves **1**
Prep time **3 minutes**

1 Using a bar spoon, carefully layer the three ingredients, in order, in a shot glass (see below).

2 Serve immediately.

## Layering

This is also referred to as pousse café. The technique involves a number of spirits and liqueurs being carefully layered, one by one, in a shot glass, and the drink is then consumed in one mouthful. It is achieved by using the flat end of a bar spoon against the surface of each liquid and works because liquids have different densities, so some will be lighter than others and will therefore float on the layers beneath.

Pour the first liquid ingredient listed in the recipe into the shot glass, being careful not to allow any on the side of the glass. Position the bar spoon in the center of the glass with the rounded part of the spoon facing toward you. The spoon should be resting against the inside of the glass while also being in contact with the first liquid ingredient. Carefully and slowly pour the second liquid ingredient down the bar spoon so that it flows into the glass along the spoon and sits on top of the first liquid, creating a second layer. Repeat with the third ingredient, then carefully remove the bar spoon.

# PIMM'S COCKTAIL

THIS IS MORE ALCOHOLIC THAN THE ORIGINAL, WITH THE ADDITION OF GIN, BUT IT'S JUST AS REFRESHING. GINGER ALE ADDS A DELICIOUS SPICINESS TO THE DRINK.

1 Fill a highball glass with ice cubes. Build all the remaining ingredients, one by one in order, over the ice.

2 Decorate with cucumber strips, blueberries, and orange wheels and serve.

ice cubes
1 measure Pimm's No 1
1 measure gin
2 measures lemonade
2 measures ginger ale
cucumber strips, blueberries, and orange wheels, to decorate

Serves **1**
Prep time **3 minutes**

# ICED **LEMON** & MINT VODKA

1 Pour the lemon juice, cordial, and vodka into a cocktail shaker and shake well.

2 Pour the cocktail into six tall glasses half-filled with ice cubes. Add a few mint sprigs and top up with tonic water. Serve immediately.

¼ cup lemon juice
½ cup lemon cordial
½ cup vodka, chilled
ice cubes
a few mint sprigs
tonic water

Serves **6**
Prep time **6 minutes**

# INDEX

# ACKNOWLEDGMENTS

**Picture Credits**
Key: a above, b below, c center, l left, r right.

Octopus Publishing Group 138, 148, 211; Stephen Conroy 18, 21, 24, 26, 29, 31, 34, 47, 63, 67, 77, 78, 79, 83, 88, 91, 104, 118, 119, 121, 127 left, 136, 141, 150, 191, 222, 224, 226, 227, 228, 229, 230, 236, 243, 245, 246; Will Heap 25, 58, 68, 127 right, 128, 130, 131, 142, 180, 189, 201, 203, 213, 215; David Jordan 49; William Lingwood 10, 30, 86, 178, 183; David Loftus 37, 61, 206, 211, 237; Jason Lowe 43, 51, 55, 71, 112, 158, 161, 167, 168, 218; David Munns 16, 120, 132; Sean Myers 117; Peter Myers 45; Emma Neish 56, 107, 108, 157, 169, 171; Lis Parsons 17, 20, 23, 27, 32, 33, 64, 65, 111; William Reavell 12, 19, 66, 99, 100, 154, 172, 173, 174, 175, 182, 187, 188, 208; Gareth Sambidge 96, 196, 197; William Shaw 15; Simon Smith 13; Ian Wallace 50, 53, 57, 59, 82, 93, 94, 122, 125, 137, 143, 144, 179, 194, 198, 216; Philip Webb 41
**Shutterstock** 38br, 42br, 74br, 87br, 92ar, 98br, 113c, 124br, 134br, 151bc, 163bl, 185br, 212bc, 219ac
Additional background images: **Thinkstock**

**Publisher** Sarah Ford
**Editor** Pauline Bache
**Features Writer** Cara Frost-Sharratt
**Designer** Eoghan O'Brien
**Layout Design** Jaz Bahra and Hugh Schermuly
**Cover Design** Jo Bell
**Picture Library Manager** Jennifer Veall
**Assistant Production Manager** Caroline Alberti
**Senior Production Manager** Peter Hunt